THE HANDS OF DESTINY

UK Leading Spiritual Healer
ANDREW McKELLAR

(known as Andy)

Diane M Homer

Dedication

By Andrew McKellar

I would like to dedicate this book to Sri Sathya Sai Baba. Thank you Swami, for all that you do for me, you have stood by me all these years. It means so much Thank You Master.

Also Mr Ted Fricker, who healed countless sufferers in his lifetime.

To the lady who wrote this book. Diane M. Homer. I knew all along she could do it. She came up trumps! An amazing lady.

Also to Geri McKellar, a truly outstanding Medium. Her work and reputation speak volumes. She is the greatest Medium since Doris Stokes.

To my children Sarah, Andrew Jnr, Marcus, Kristie-Anne: a big thank you.

To Marcus for designing the book cover and all the other work he does for me.

To my spirit doctors: Dr Williams, Dr Cotton.

Finally, to Mr Isaac Tigret, founder of the Hardrock Café and House of Blues. A truly amazing man who has given so much of himself to the Master and to the Cause of Spirituality.

Knowing him has had a great impact on my life.

Sai Ram Isaac.

Contents

Chapter

Acknowledgement

I wish to thank the patients who have given permission for the publication of their problems within this book, which in turn will enable others to see that they too can follow their footpath to the Healing Sanctuary and be the receivers of Andy's truly amazing healing.

Namely:

BRIAN	*ALAN*	*GAYLE*
CAROLE	*KIM* *USA*	*LES*
G.P.	*MATT*	*ALISON* *USA*
GENTLEMAN *USA*	*ANN* *MAJORCA*	*CAROLE*
LINDA *MAJORCA*	*G.P.* *GUERNSEY*	*HARRY*
GENTLEMAN	*SANDRA*	*SHERRY*
VICKY	*NICK*	*JANE*
MATT	*LEE*	*VINCE*

FREIDA	STEVE	TERRY
ALAN	LADY	BRUCE USA
MICK	FAY	BERYL
TREVOR	LIANNE	LES
LISA	WARREN	STEVE G.P.
GAIL	DAVID	DAVID'S WIFE
GENTLEMAN	IAN	LES
FRAN	PAT	SUE
HOLLY	BOBBY	LADY
KATY	CRAIG	GENTLEMAN
STEVE		

There are many more patients I am sure who would have also given testimonials if approached, but I feel that this selection will give you an indication of the diverse range of illnesses which have been treated very successfully by Andy. Thousands more I am sure would have been delighted to have added their stories.

Chapter 1

Introducing Andrew McKellar

Andy was born on the 21st November 1962, the elder of two step-brothers, Michael and Kenny. His father Malcolm was a chef in the Merchant Navy and spent many months away from his family, but his nickname was Jock as he was in fact a Scotsman. His mother's name was Maureen, who worked as a Catering Assistant at Southampton Docks in the 60s era. Life was very hard during this period, as for many families, and consequently they moved seven times in a very short space of time, but eventually settled in Warren Crescent, in the Shirley Warren area of Southampton. Andy attended the local Shirley Warren state schools within the area and was sometimes reluctant in this respect, as he found school situations difficult.

Andrew unfortunately did not know his grandparents on his father's side and is always keen to point out that in fact the person whom he related to as his father was not in fact his real father. He had left his mother when she became pregnant with Andrew and subsequently she went on to marry his stepfather and had two further sons. His maternal grandparents unfortunately he did not see except for a few times during his life, and I am sure deep down inside it must have been very hurtful for Andrew and one which he possibly has hidden deep in his soul. These are experiences which children bury inside their hearts, always leaving the question unanswered – 'why?'.

Andy and his family were animal lovers and their cats were very much part of the integral home. To this day Andy loves his pets and as many clients know his Dove accompanies him in his sanctuary. Such a beautiful sign of peace and love!

When Andy was a young man in his teens he had quite a few experiences which gradually unfolded and which to him at that young age were explainable yet intriguing, and he became aware of other entities in his life that were totally different from anything that he had envisaged before.

Other than that Andy led the normal teenage life, spending time with his friends, enjoying swimming and cycling and messing around as they all do at that age. He loved music and played the harmonica, carrying on to learn the guitar, which he plays extremely well to this day and certainly he is a gifted musician with an amazing voice. He was very intrigued by the music of Elvis Presley and certainly has the voice to match this style of singing. Another gift which has seen him through many difficult times I am sure.

His style of course was that of a Teddy Boy, as they were called in those days. He dressed accordingly, sporting a quiff hairdo, wearing a bootlace with his shirts, the drapes and the winkle picker shoes. He acquired the full dress code, of which he was extremely proud. If you were not sporting this style of clothes you would have been considered a Mod who drove a scooter of the day, or a Square who wore brogue shoes, 50s and 60s lingo, so to speak! Of course, as everyone knows only too well, Teddy Boys used to go around in gangs and at times this led to various experiences which I daresay Andy would prefer to forget. Unfortunately the culture was that you could not be seen as shirking your responsibilities within a group of male Teddy Boys, and so he followed the sheep, so to speak. The bravado of the young!

During his life he has overcome extreme hardship on numerous occasions, far more than he can ever account for, and partly because they are too painful for him to comprehend. He has seen and experienced things which no young person should ever have to see, yet alone live through. However during these times he did not realise that they would stand him in good stead for his main role in life, that of a healer of others.

Andy himself is a very sensitive person and I truly believe these experiences have had a profound effect on his relationships and his devotion to his patients, whom he can relate directly with on many areas, including illnesses.

He lacked communication skills from a very young age which in turn he had to overcome. In other words he saw the world far from the rose-tinted glasses aspect, but instead witnessed cruelty and violence which occurred away from prying eyes on a regular basis.

At one of his lowest ebbs and just managing to keep himself going and not being dragged down an undesirable pathway, he was aware of these dreams and of other entities entering his life far more than before, and somehow he felt at peace with himself and gradually became more and more conscious that in fact things were beginning to look up and he was beginning to open up his eyes and see a future unfolding before him which he dared not comprehend on one hand, yet curious on another. What was happening, and where was he going to be stepping to in the future?

During one of these periods of awareness it came to him that he was going to become one of a number of chosen people who would be able to help others in a very significant way. Then he wondered, why me? Is this truly happening or am I imagining hearing these declarations in my head? Lo and behold, they were not just figments of the imagination. The opportunities gradually unfolded.

Chapter 2

Andy's spiritual experiences in childhood

Andy's gifts were with him from birth. As a young child he was very aware of spiritual happenings and assumed that everyone experienced the same phenomena. He would sense people around him and also feel their presence, experiencing tingling sensations, warmth and feelings of calmness and was at one with himself.

Andy is extremely sensitive to others, and through the years his vulnerability has remained with him, which as you can imagine has been hard for him at times to cope with life. Spirit would appear to Andy and he felt their guidance on many occasions. Apart from his silent visitors, his out of body experiences gradually increased from around the age of six. During these times he would be surrounded by lights in beautiful colours – some flickering around the room and shooting across from wall to wall. A feeling of calmness would ascend around him. In simple terms this can happen when you are lying down and you feel as though you are floating on a magic carpet – taking you up through the ceiling, where you find yourself hovering above the tree line, over house tops to travel beyond. It can be a very exciting experience. Other times, when looking into glass mirrors, he could see a beautiful glow of light surrounding his body. It was comforting in the knowledge that it made him feel safe somehow, but he was unable to understand the meaning behind it. He just could not explain why this happened to him, although he always knew his spiritual friends were safeguarding him.

In the evening time there was one person who appeared where he was able to make out the shape of a man's body. This person was tall with an eye patch covering one eye – possibly 40 years of age. He remained in his life till his early teens. Other spiritual friends came also. I am sure in some ways this was a great solace to him. Especially as he himself wondered why it was that his other siblings did not have any inkling about spiritual beings, and he often pondered the question 'why me?'

Through the years it became extremely hard for Andy to be taken seriously by his parents, who just dismissed his experiences. In particular, his father had an extremely controlling personality and totally ignored the 'goings on', so to speak, which surrounded his son. He much preferred, as the saying goes, "sweeping it under the carpet", as was often the case in those times. He was far more interested in sport on the television than listening to his son, who so wished to share his experiences with him. Alas, it was not to be. It was perceived that his son had a very vivid imagination and was slightly odd.

With all these unexplainable situations occurring, Andy must have felt quite isolated at not being able to converse with his father, as deep down he really wished to have a common bond with him, but alas, this was not meant to be. It must have been so disheartening.

14

Chapter 3

Home Life

Andy's childhood was in the era of "Children should be seen but not heard". I am sure that there are many of us who can relate to those times, and for a child who was very sensitive, it would have been very hurtful. His mother was extremely caring of her offspring, and I would like to mention at this point that life was indeed not easy for her or the children.

As a young child Andy suffered abuse from his father when he returned from his trips to sea. Incidentally, he was not a drinker as one might assume, but he had a foul temper and would physically beat him, which included the use of belts and anything he could lay his hands on. His father would strike out at times for no apparent reason, and as you can imagine at such a young age Andy could hardly speak as he was so traumatised by all these events, and was therefore totally isolated in his own world.

When he was only two and a half years of age, his father beat him up severely one Saturday morning. His sibling would rock his cot, pushing the carpet close to the door, so his father and mother became very angry because Andy could not open the door (bearing in mind his age). He was then told to go to the window and lift the latch so his father could climb up and get through the window. This he then did, but when his father ascended up the ladder and into the room he then began (after removing his belt) to beat Andy with it on the top of his leg and in turn the buckle tore down into it, which resulted in a two-inch gash, which had blood pouring from the wound profusely. His leg felt very weak, and his hands were covered in blood. He was then thrown into his parents' bedroom. Eventually his father decided that he should take him to the hospital, where he received stitches to his wound. This is still very vivid in Andy's mind, and it is rather disturbing that such a terrible event has had such an impact upon his life to this day, but Andy believes that suffering makes you stronger in the long run and I agree that in many situations this is the case.

As a result of this cruelty Andy developed a serious speech impediment. He became absolutely terrified of his father. Hardly surprising! It obviously has had a profound affect upon him. It was so awful for such a young child to endure. We can only imagine how he and his siblings must have felt.

At the age of five, Andy's speech became such that he had developed a really bad stutter, and he found communication extremely difficult, which in turn caused even more stress. He started having epileptic fits. In his young mind, it must have been very frightening not really knowing what was indeed happening to his own body. As you can imagine, this ignited the situation even further. There was this young child experiencing such cruelty, and health issues in turn were making him very vulnerable on the outside, being teased, laughed at and bullied by his peers. It is so hard to comprehend the hardships some children have to endure, and Andy was one of these.

17

Chapter 4

An Interlude: happier times – Aged 10 years

On a lighter note, I am going to recall a happier event which Andy experienced when he was asked to attend a school camp in the New Forest. It was a child's dream of freedom, adventure, fresh air and being able to run free in the fields and paddle in the streams in wellington boots. I'm sure we can all relate to this in some form or another. It was a chance for a child living in a city environment, where it was so built up, suddenly having the opportunity to experience a holiday in the countryside, and it must have been truly wonderful for Andy.

However, there was one source of apprehension, which related to the PE teacher who had been given authority to take charge of the trip, as at that time Andy was not much of an athlete as far as sporting activities were concerned. Opportunities were very limited in the city, and he dreaded having to participate in games as he did not want to appear 'stupid'. Possibly his sensitivity and shyness played a great part in how he perceived himself to be inadequate, to participate in sport, and therefore he did not want to bring attention to himself. Many of us, I am sure, can relate to these experiences ourselves during our early years.

The camp site was in a beautiful area of the New Forest in Hampshire. Here wild horses, wild boar, foxes and other wildlife were in abundance during these years, and the scenery there to this day is absolutely magnificent, especially for a young child like Andy who had never had such an experience before. It would have been beyond his wildest dreams to have the chance to get out of the city and see all these amazing animals and all that countryside.

There was an added advantage, as this camping site was within the farmland and house of the teacher's parents. It was ideal also if there was an emergency, which as we all know could occur at any time when a lot of children are gathered together.

The farmer himself announced to the children that there was a young calf who had very disturbing behavioural problems. After some thought, Andy came to the conclusion that he could help this young calf and with that, at the tender age of 10 years of age, he took it into his own hands to do something to help this animal, as he felt a strong connection to it. So he walked across, lifted the latch on the gate and began walking over towards the young calf. As he did so, the calf decided to roll over, as it had been lying down at the time. After placing his hands on the calf for a while, he gently started stroking it, and then decided to put his arms around, comforting her, knowing that this was exactly what she so desperately needed. Such awareness on Andy's part.

Unbeknown to Andy, the teacher had made his parents aware of the events unfolding before his very eyes, so they too stood and watched and even decided to record the event on camera. They were delighted to experience at first hand the gentleness and healing Andy had given the animal, totally transforming its previous behaviour. Andy himself must have felt the inner glow and knew strongly that he could help this young calf. It must have been quite a revelation to him at the time to know that his skill was being acknowledged at long last, and by complete strangers.

The following year the trip was organised yet again to visit the farm and Andy was offered a place free of charge, as the farming family had been so delighted with the outcome of the calf. However, his father totally refused his permission for Andy to attend, which in turn left a very saddened and disappointed child.

Chapter 5

Health Issues

Andy was plagued with misfortune healthwise, resulting in several serious and debilitating medical conditions:

(a) Serious speech impediment

Andy's belief is that his father was overly strict with him and therefore he was terrified of him. Hence, the stammer. When he was with his own friends, he felt more secure and the stammer was noticeably less. However, not to be deterred as he grew older and with all the spiritual awakenings he was experiencing, he became convinced that he could teach himself to speak like everybody else. Slowly and with great determination, he succeeded in so doing over the period of one year.

Imagine the relief this must have brought him, as well as boosting his confidence after spending years and years feeling worthless, inadequate, unable to communicate positively and express his feelings with others, having felt total isolation from life in general. No child should have to feel this way, but as we all know, this is still going on to this day for many of them.

(b) Epilepsy

Moving on now after years of suffering various symptoms, it was finally acknowledged by the medical profession that he did in fact have epilepsy. As we are all fully aware, this has devastating effects on the whole body. It is not the fits themselves, but the profound tiredness which is experienced as a result of all the drugs for nausea and muscle weaknesses etc. There is also experienced a constant brain block, which causes even more anxiety to the patient.

Andy was fully aware of how his life would continue, having seen many situations with others at first hand. He was determined not to live his life in this way and at the tender age of 16 he decided to throw all his medication in the rubbish bin. His mother was mortified and got in touch with the G.P. for the local area. Andy attended an appointment and was told in a grave manner that he would be in serious trouble by the age of 20 if he were to continue on this pathway. However, to date Andy has only ever had two fits, which incidentally were in close succession, and he has had no other repercussions in over 35 years, having taking it into his own hands, so to speak, and being silently determined to cure himself of these fits. Remarkable! Andy did achieve his goal!

On a slightly different note, it took Andy years to convince the medical profession that he was fully fit to drive, but he was very persistent, and won his case at the age of 29 years. Now that's determination!

Chapter 6

Gaining Confidence about his own capabilities

Andy's inner strength was gaining momentum, and as time passed he knew his spiritual beings were guiding him forward in ways he could never have imagined. His confidence was growing and his fears were beginning to subside. He had the comfort of knowing that with each step he was taking, his spiritual friends were around him and guiding him.

Chapter 7

Various incidents involving Andy's spiritual awareness from a young child

(a) Cycling

Andy was riding his bicycle down a steep hill onto a very busy road, and he was having to turn right; he glanced behind him and his vision was clear, when an extremely loud voice entered his head and said "Don't pull out Andrew, and don't turn right". So Andrew decided in a split second to keep left and obey the voice. With that a car appeared travelling at high speed, and there was no doubt left in his mind that he would have been killed if he had not heeded those words.

(b) Wanting answers

In time, he decided to approach some of his teachers to obtain their views and ideas and their thoughts on what he could be perceived to do in the future, as he himself was convinced that he would be 'world famous'. There was no rhyme nor reason for this except a knowingness deep down inside him.

At the age of 12, he approached his father yet again, who in turn suggested that he needed to meet with a psychiatrist, who would indeed have a different perspective on the matter. Andy found himself being rejected yet again. Not the ideal situation for one so young, who was trying desperately to obtain his father's attention, which he obviously craved.

24

Chapter 8

Andy's Grandmother

At around the age of 13 Andy received the news that his grandmother had passed away. Although he had hardly seen her during his life, he had very fond memories of her, describing her as a sweet old lady. As a result of her passing, his Uncle Brian inherited her home with his family. He was her son.

On one specific occasion when Andy was 14 he was approached to be a babysitter by the uncle. One particular evening when both children were sleeping and were tucked up in bed, Andy was alone downstairs in the house and had decided to go and check on the children when suddenly he became aware that the door handle was in the down position and the door was gradually opening. He reached across before it could retract, and grabbed the door and opened it wide. There was no one there.

His uncle's pet Collie dog was sitting at the bottom of the stairs with her hackles up and whimpering. There was no other sound at all. So he descended the stairs to comfort the dog, who was obviously still distressed.

Andy himself was shaken but not frightened, and upon his Uncle's return he discussed with him what had indeed occurred whilst he was out, and said he believed that it was his grandmother in spirit. He received an extremely negative response and was warned not to tell anyone at all of the occurrence. I can understand his frustration at others' attitudes

– I have come across this negativity as well on various occasions. However in time it was proved that in fact his intuition was 100% correct.

On one particular day, just as he was leaving his uncle's house yet again, he looked back and saw that his grandmother had just walked past him and back into the house. She was within three feet of him or thereabouts, looking exactly the same as she always had when bidding farewell. She walked through the hallway and turned off to the kitchen. Andy was intrigued, and decided to trace his steps back into the house. The lights were off and he then decided to turn them on, but there was nothing to be seen.

Upon sharing this experience with his mother, she again dismissed it. Her reply was "Andrew, let my mother rest in peace". His father's input was yet again negative. However, a few weeks later whilst his father was away again at sea, the inevitable realisation occurred, in relation to his mother, who came knocking on his door in earnest at 1 am, looking extremely worried and white-faced, her whole body trembling, and she was pointing to her bedroom. Finally she said, "Mum's here". She had been sleeping when she was awoken suddenly, and there was her mother standing in front of her at the bedroom door. Although in the past she may not have wanted to acknowledge the facts, she could not dismiss what she was experiencing directly in front of her.

This realisation of what Andy had been trying to share with her from a very young age was to change her mindset forever, which in turn gradually brought them closer and closer together. The irony was that he saw his grandmother now far more than during her earthly life.

Andy's mother was indeed a very kind soul, quiet and unassuming, and Andy would become very close to her. In time she became very supportive of his beliefs. A complete turnaround of circumstances. Personally I believe it was fear of her husband before this event which put a wedge between her and her son.

There is a picture which has pride of place in the Healing Room – Maureen – Mother of Andy. Taken to the other side, so to speak, before her time.

Fear is something Andy has little of through suffering so much in life and he is now a strong, powerful being – you can see the power in his eyes. A man filled with love, he fears no man or beast, and does not suffer fools gladly.

He says "I was born to heal, and that is exactly what I do. Many have scorned me, even doctors have chastised my work on TV shows. But no fool will stand in my way ever, my work is superior to medical science, and always has been and always will be. They need to open their minds. Medical science is still in its infancy. They have so much to learn – they know so little, bless them."

Chapter 9

A tragic accident

Next, there was an occasion when his uncle himself was to experience such a phenomenon, when his younger son Tony was involved in a tragic motorbike accident. He received fatal skull injuries and did not stand a chance of survival. The whole family were devastated. However, not long afterwards whilst Andy was at home the young lad came and said 'Andy, I'm going to move the boxes in the loft. Also, can you tell my dad that the black dog was hit but it was not killed'. On speaking to his uncle privately to discuss the unfolding events, his uncle seemed very perplexed, but did however admit that his wife's brother had accidentally driven into a black Labrador dog, which had lived. The uncle left, still sceptical however once again, an attitude which was indeed going to change radically in a short space of time.

His uncle telephoned, very excited, yet apprehensive to tell Andy what he had recently experienced, saying, 'You're not going to believe what has happened" and stating that his loft was locked. It was not possible for anyone to get up there. Furthermore, he and his aunt had been lying in bed the other evening when they had heard movement in the loft. Tony's belongings had gone up there in boxes after he had died and had masking tape on them to seal them tight. When it stopped he decided to investigate, and found that the boxes were all open and all the toys etc. were scattered over the floor. There were small footprints in the dust up there too!

Andy stated that he believed that 'there is no such thing as death – you cannot die'. Brian this time believed him totally.

Chapter 10

Medium – young Tony makes his presence known

We cast our minds forward now to an event which Andy attended at Southampton Guildhall, where the Welsh Medium Stephen O'Brian was appearing to a wide audience. Andy marvelled at his expertise on the subject.

After a short time, Andy was to experience a spotlight appearing directly above his head and Stephen was saying "I have a young boy here. He suffered an impact to his head. Oh dear, it was a terrible impact being hit by a motorbike. He's dancing, saying '"I'm not dead – I'm still alive" and he is combing his hair in a teddy boy quiff. Is his name Tony? He's saying "you used to comb his hair into this quiff. He's saying 'comb my hair like yours' and now he is saying 'you haven't got any windows!' Can that be right? Do you understand?"

Andy certainly did. His Uncle Brian's young son, who was incidentally so sadly missed, was making contact again. Andy was the only person who could possibly relate to the incidences.

The statement 'no windows' made absolute sense. His home was being modernised at the time and the windows had been removed. Young Tony was joyous at be able to communicate to his Uncle.

Chapter 11

Learning and understanding how to use his gifts

As the years unfolded Andy realised that his life was not ever going to be the 'norm', so to speak. That no matter how much he wanted it to be so, his family would never understand this desire of his of wanting to help others, and also animals, and his knowingness of being attuned to the gifts which he knew he had been given within his hands.

At these times I feel he must have felt extremely isolated from society as a whole, as spiritual and psychic abilities were extremely frowned upon and can be at times even to this day in various areas. However, negativity is disappearing as awareness takes hold and people are opening up their minds to alternative health therapies. Also, more and more are gradually becoming aware of the opportunities which are on offer, and which indeed, have been around for thousands of years in some cases.

Having the foresight, and witnessing far more in dreams and realities as he stumbled through his teenage years, Andy's awareness of spiritual matters was becoming a huge part of his daily routine. Proving very challenging indeed, as all types of experiences were opening up as he began to move into the light of these events. I myself feel that Andy at this time would have been asking himself:

Who am I really?
Interpreting events which were taking place in
my dream state?
How subtle should I be?
Last but not least – where do I start?
Yes, Me! Andrew McKellar!

Contemplating his life, Andy was fully aware already of situations and difficulties being experienced by his peers via his dreams, and the knowledge passed to him by his sensory beings, who were forever present and showing him all the things which will be evolving in his life.

It was a great comfort to him.

Chapter 12

17 years old

As Andy became 17 years of age, it occurred to him that in fact he had had no parental advice or direction given in what career he should pursue, and which direction he should take, and he decided to take it into his own hands and look for work. Andy has a very artistic side to his personality and so he decided that he would like to take an apprenticeship with a sign writer, and this he achieved.

However, this time his father was extremely excited that his son had now taken steps to (in his mind) achieve stable work, and therefore be able to support himself totally. His attitude changed towards his son. However, it was to be short lived, as after only three weeks in the apprenticeship Andy became very unwell due to the fumes he was exposed to every day, and realised that this was not the right occupation for him, bearing in mind his epilepsy. He knew the only answer was to leave the apprenticeship, knowing full well the consequences of his actions in relation to his father. As you can already assume, he was not best pleased, his attitude being that his son was stupid, and he stated that he had now lost all respect for him.

Andy and his siblings had over many years been told "the only jobs you will ever be good for are sweeping the roads". So this had a disastrous effect on them all and they had begun to believe same, and were convinced that they were not worthy in any way of pleasing their father, ever.

It was decided therefore by his father, as he was so ashamed of him, that he would kick Andy out of the house and onto the streets, at the tender age of 17 years. How devastating this must have been after everything he had endured throughout the years, since a very young age at the hands of his father. It does not condone this type of outcome whatsoever. Imagine how we would have felt in the circumstances! Struggling throughout your childhood with all those horrendous situations, health issues and then to find yourself out on the streets - it does not bear thinking about!

Take a moment and contemplate this, and then take note that when you encounter a young lad on the streets, he too may have a story to tell which may not be so dissimilar to Andy's. Keep an open mind, and do not judge whoever you may see. They made need your kindness too!

Andy's motto, which he lives by, the words of Sri Sathya Sai Baba:

Love All, Serve All

Chapter 13

Homelessness

How devastated Andy must have felt, finding himself living hand to mouth out on the streets. As a result, he began drinking heavily, as he believed this would give him the confidence which by this time in his life he was so lacking. The weekends became a total haze of booze. He found himself reduced to living in woodland areas, sleeping under bushes, in old garages etc. you name it he has done it!

Sometimes he would prise corrugated iron off old buildings to use as shelter, and sleep on floorboards. He was totally alone, and in actual fact in all he spent about two to three years living this way of life, just wishing to be totally alone. He was unable to sign on as he was "of no fixed abode" and at this time his epilepsy still figured in his life. He believed himself to be totally and utterly worthless.

In time, Andy however found that he could pick up the odd painting and decorating jobs through the courtesy of some of his friends, doing up bedsitters which were in need of a facelift.

Chapter 14

New beginnings

After a while Andy met a girl, and he gradually came to the conclusion that he should put in more effort to fit in, and then they both decided to get an application form for a council flat. They were lucky enough to be chosen. As time went on marriage followed, and he became a father to two children, Sarah and Andrew, but alas it did not last and Andy has no hesitation in taking full responsibility in that respect, caused due to his own insecurities at that time.

He is still in contact with Sarah and Andrew Jnr. In his own words "I always will be. They are my children, I love them".

Chapter15

Wayward trends returned as he became very unhappy

Andy's long-term relationship had broken down and once again he found himself having to move on and set up a new place for himself, taking with him his beloved copy of "Phone calls from the Dead".

Once again, Andy began lapsing back into drinking heavily and at weekends staying with friends. Andy was totally devastated. He had now reached rock bottom. He found himself yet again on a downward spiral and decided to take his own life, as he believed he had nothing to live for. Andy decided to take a rope and go to Southampton Common, where he would proceed to hang himself – in sheer and total desperation.

As he was contemplating his next move however, he heard a voice say loud and clear "Andrew, don't do this, you are one of a chosen few". Then he received a vision which showed masses of people coming towards him – literally pushing their way forward, saying "Help me, Help me!" Andy was totally overwhelmed by this time, and he thought, "How can I help these people when I cannot even help myself?"

Having pondered on this, he decided to take no action in relation to his suicide bid. He had begun to question his own vulnerability at this time, and dismissed all negative thoughts and decided to move forward in his life instead, and see what the future did in fact hold for him.

Chapter 16

A change of lifestyle

A while later at a party, Andy was talking to a young man who had approached him and who then started talking about life after death. He suggested to Andy that he should attend a Spiritualist Church and get involved on this pathway. This he did, and attended the Spiritualist Church in Grove Road, Shirley, Southampton.

On his very first visit he decided that he would sit at the back out of sight (so he thought) from the medium up on stage. However, that was not what happened! The medium called out, "You have been through a heck of a lot, young man. You have contemplated taking your own life. Everything you have been through has been a test. Do you realise who you are? You have been born for a special purpose. You are going to become Britain's most famous Healer. You are going to be the next Harry Edwards". Andy had no idea whatsoever who Harry Edwards was, or anything relating to his life's work.

Andy was now 23 years of age. He was jobless, separated from his wife and children and it was also winter. He thought about what had been said. He found it very difficult to comprehend, as at that time he had great difficulty in understanding the majority of people and felt quite isolated. Therefore he could not imagine himself being a Healer. Obviously for him it felt very unreal, especially as at the time he was suffering with severe depression, and was yet again living in sub-standard accommodation, which incidentally was much better than on the streets.

In Victorian times, Derby Road, the area in which he found himself living, had been considered a highly respectable area, and the properties were very sought after. Alas, now they are frequented by those less fortunate and the buildings are crumbling into disrepair.

Andy looked around his attic room and with foresight decided to strip it all out and painted the walls etc., and with a lot of elbow grease he could see at last the end result of a job well done. He was in a safe environment and he found he could relax again, and at last began to feel uplifted and thankful for this roof over his head and to feel he was gaining stability.

After a short while he began hearing some very odd noises. He learned also that the previous tenants had not stayed very long in this room due to weird happenings. There was obviously a problem which the Landlord had neglected to share with his new tenant. Andy decided that he would start to purchase some spiritual books and widen his knowledge and take new steps towards opening up his mind to new spheres, the unknown.

One evening whilst reading quietly, he could sense heavy breathing in the middle of the room. He searched around as the breathing was getting louder. He continued checking the balcony, everywhere – nothing. The breathing was still getting louder and louder. Totally frustrated and bewildered, he decided to have a word and blurted out, "I recognise your presence".

With that it immediately stopped. On looking back, he realises it was in fact consolidation of his spiritual growth, being a much larger part of his life than he had previously thought.

These psychic events were here to stay, and his adult life was now being more committed to spiritual growth as his mediumistic awareness unfolded, and his intuition was far greater than the norm, so to speak. His belief was such that somehow he began to realise he too could take the stage as a medium in a Spiritual Church environment. Although, yet again the old 'self-doubt' resurged.

In time, Andy's personal belief grew within himself, and his inner intuition was that he knew he had to take heed of the words that had been given to him by the medium. Gradually his life began to unfold, slowly but positively towards a brighter existence.

Chapter 17

Healing Awareness
Now Andy's life was really unfolding

Andy decided to purchase a book about Harry Edwards, who incidentally ran the Harry Edwards Sanctuary in Shere, Surrey. It stands in grounds of great beauty appreciated by many to this day.

Upon reading through the chapters of outstanding phenomena, which began from Harry's early manhood in the 1930s until his timely passing in 1976, he had devoted his whole life into helping others using his healing gifts and became an international legend in his time. Through these accounts Andy became fully aware of the gift which he himself had had bestowed upon him from birth, which was indeed very precious and made him feel very humble.

Ted Fricker, who was also a healer, became the person who would have the greatest effect on young Andy. He felt a great urge of expectation on meeting him and he too had had numerous experiences in his childhood which Andy was able to relate too. Ted was not religious in any way.

A number of years later, Andy left his body and had a real life 'out of body' experience and met Ted. He took his hand and said, "you are destined to do this work for the rest of your life, just as I did". It was then that he began to take his spiritual path seriously.

Andy therefore decided to attend the Spiritual Church again. There was at that time a lady called Rose who took him under her wing, so to speak. Rose herself was a novice at the time in spiritual matters. Later the inevitable happened and they became very close and formed a strong relationship which lasted for some 10 years. During this time Andy's life became far more stable. He took on small contracts working for a painting company, social services and a boat mast manufacturer.

During these years he was still very aware of being surrounded by spiritual beings and they were always present. In some of the first instances Andy was convinced that he had burglars until after the incident, then realisation set in that all was well and that in fact it was spiritual involvement within the home.

Another time when Andy and Rose were modernising their home and were in fact resting in bed, they heard someone kicking the door. He scrambled out of bed, taking a piece of discarded wood left by the workmen in his hand as a safeguard, and opened the door. To his dismay he saw no one at all out on the landing, and thought that maybe this person was in the other room across the way. Listening, he could hear boxes being moved across the floor and others being placed around the room. At this point of time Andy was beginning to get agitated (as anyone would in this type of situation). He opened the door, fully believing he would come face to face with the intruder (switching the light on as he went), only to discover that in fact it was empty but all his possessions were scattered across the floor in no particular order – how absurd! No one could have passed him, as he was standing in the only escape route. There was no rhyme or reason for such an event.

Having discussed the incident with Rose, it was decided that this room would become a healing room and be a place of peace and tranquillity. Personally, I believe it was a jolt for Andy to sit up and take notice and get on with changing the energies of the room so he could progress with his healing work.

From this moment on Andy was inundated with clients. They came from all different walks of life, a complete cross-section of nationalities. Some of them were generous with their donations and others not so. Usual story of life as I know it! At this time Andy was also maintaining a part time job as well, to make ends meet so to speak. So his life became extremely busy, to say the least.

Chapter 18

Control

The first lesson of this came through the following experience. Having completed a full-on day of healing work, and remembering from hindsight that it was late afternoon and Rose was clutching a watering can, Andy was descending down the outside staircase when he turned and suddenly hit the floor. He knew it was totally different from an epileptic fit and felt more like he had been drugged.

Managing to come to, and drag himself to his bed, he collapsed on the top, boots as well, and managed to cover himself up in the quilt – nothing could make him move, he felt totally exhausted. Then all of a sudden he could hear breathing in his right ear. He was petrified, unable to open his eyes, and, being totally aware of his physical form, he remembers that he recited the Lord's Prayer, at the same time thinking, "what a hypocrite!"

Then he was aware of a pair of hands moving through the quilt and being placed onto his lower abdomen. He felt the warmth from the fingers. They remained for a few seconds, and then slowly began moving up until they were on his throat. By this time he was really panicking, and at this point was able to hear this audible voice say, as though sensing his fear, "We are not here to harm you, my child, we are here to help you. You must control the healing energies. You must not overwork your own energies. You could slip into a coma and die". It had lasted no more than a couple of minutes and with that Andy fell asleep right through until 8 am the next morning. He slept for 14 solid hours.

He continued to generate more and more clients, as he had become well established and was known for having this absolutely amazing life-changing energy, which he was totally the guardian of.

Of course in these matters there are always ups and downs and for Andy too, there are no exceptions. To keep continuing down his chosen pathway, he attended a development group at Grove Road, which had been recommended to him, but he found it very discerning as it did not involve constructive views and criticisms. Also, the people sitting in the groups themselves were not attaining the results of awareness they should have achieved after a certain amount of time. There was also a phenomenal amount of jealousy as well. Andy became very disillusioned, and he is not one to hold back in coming forward, and believes in getting straight to the point always and stating things as they are, no frivolous creeping! I must admit, I myself prefer this logic. You know exactly where you stand. So the door was then closed in this regard.

At the same time, however, the Southampton Echo was following his progress with great interest, and its readers were becoming more and more interested in this young man who was dedicating his life to "helping his fellow man to gain good health and strength," and not charging an exorbitant fee but taking donations instead. There are not many people who would have done this, as we all know only too well. This in itself speaks volumes about his integrity as a human being.

Chapter 19

America – First visit

Andy was relaxing one day on the bed when he heard a voice telling him "Andrew – go to America". It was repeated 3-4 times, which made him sit up and take notice, as previously he had had no desire whatsoever to visit the US.

Within a few days, he received a long-distance call from the States, from Winter Haven in Florida, from friends he knew as Jill and Graham, offering him an open invitation to meet Bill Anchor, Minister of the Science of Spirituality Organisation. Andy and Rose decided to accept the invitation, as at the back of his mind he remembered the voice incident previously.

On arrival he was introduced to Bill Anchor, who was suffering with neck and knee issues, and Andy obliged and offered him healing, which he duly accepted and which turned out to be a great success.

Then Andy was approached in relation to giving a talk to a few people during his visit, and duly obliged yet again. It was to be held at the Minister's home. However, word leaked out and around 80 people arrived, and the event was a great success.

The following day people were arriving and asking for healing. This was not quite the holiday Andy had envisaged.

A memorable experience

There was one particular case which has remained close to Andy's heart, and that was of a young baby of eight months, who had a tumour throughout the stomach region and obviously was crying and very distressed. Andy placed his hands over the area and the baby became calmer and calmer and began to relax. The swelling began subsiding and the baby was able to wear a proper diaper within a short time. The tumour had completely gone and the consultant was dumbfounded.

Andy remained humble, but at the same time proud to have been able to help. He realised also that his visit was indeed a great success as he continued to see more patients. The support and kindness received from everyone was overwhelming.

Chapter 20

American – second visit

On this occasion Andy received a great honour when he was ordained as a Minister of the Science and Spirituality Organisation, in recognition of his healing gift and the contribution he made in this respect on his first visit.

Andy was very impressed with their open-minded attitude and their thirst for learning about his field of work. The Americans' attitude continues to this day, not to dismiss what you do not understand but to explore all possibilities rather than standing still in a negative mode, and dismissing anything which they do not understand, which is very much the attitude here in the UK, although saying that, in the last two years I am beginning to see a light at the end of the tunnel and a gradual increase of enquiring minds at last! It must have been so refreshing for Andy.

Chapter 21

Sathya Sai Baba Healing

The experiences and apparitions which have taken place over the years for Andy are truly amazing. In his own words, "I have no religion as such, apart from Sathya Sai Baba," whom he visited in India whilst still living with Rose.

His Indian Guru, Bhagavan Sri Sathya Sai Baba, known to millions of devotees throughout the world, is deemed to be the God Incarnate, his name being a combination of "Truth" (Sathya) and "Divine Mother and Father" (Sai Baba). He is a spiritual phenomenon of the highest order. Andy became very interested in everything that he had read and heard about him, and when a friend suggested going to India, he did not hesitate.

This was Andy's first experience of travelling to India. He found it extremely exciting as it was totally unfamiliar to that of his own country. He boarded a plane at Heathrow, travelling to Bangalore and then by taxi from there to Puttapartie. This must have been quite a hair-raising experience.

Having arrived, he decided to go straight to the Ashram, after all this is what he had come for. Andy found himself sitting cross-legged on the floor in the front row and he could feel the energy filling the whole area with Omnipresence, which he found truly amazing, and the peace which filled the whole area would be hard to put into words. He learnt first-hand about his aspirations, and the pathway which he himself was taking, and wished to soak up all the vibrant energy and bask in the moment, so to speak.

Puttapartie had in fact been a very small village some years ago, but now had changed out of all recognition as thousands of followers now flocked there to get help for themselves, family members and others and listen to the teachings of Sathya Sai Baba, study his books and learn of all the aspirations that he foretold.

Subsequently Andy made another visit which he again thoroughly enjoyed which was indeed very similar to the previous one.

I am going to refrain from writing more at this point as Andy in fact made a third visit, which is very significant to me.

Chapter 22

New beginnings – Marriage

Andy had by this time in his life met and married a very beautiful lady by the name of Geri. In her own right she is a very learned scholar in relation to Buddhist teachings, having studied it in great depth for many years, and is also a medium of great renown. A very gentle, soft, caring lady whose energy in turn relates well with Andy's chosen pathway.

Geri in fact had a vision which revealed that they would indeed travel to India together, and also take a chosen group with them. Andy was sceptical as he himself had envisaged that he would not return after his last visit. However, Sathya Sai Baba had other plans, and I too found myself being asked to join the group. I felt very privileged to be travelling with everyone, especially as my desire to visit India and experience the culture had been top on my priority list since I was young.

Other members of the group and I all flew to Amsterdam and then on to Bombay. We were meeting up there with Geri and Andy when they arrived. The hustle and bustle of the streets and the immense heat were a huge contrast in relation to our summers. In fact, it was just at the end of the rainy season and there were huge muddy areas and many holes, making driving pretty treacherous, and terrifying sometimes for the passengers, including me when using transport. I do believe to this day that the traffic is as chaotic as it was then. Certainly not for the faint hearted!

The first evening was spent in a small Ashram, very simple, just the bare essentials to say the least, but clean. We decided to take a stroll through the crowded streets. There were so many people just living beside the road under awnings of plastic sheets and blankets, rugs etc., whatever material they could gather together to keep off the sun, and to huddle under when the temperature was extremely high. The children were just playing with sticks and stones, and the thing I realised very quickly was that these kiddies were so happy, smiling, laughing and enjoying themselves. A complete contrast to here in the UK. The total lack of not hearing, whingeing and whining, or "I want this" or "I want that" just did not exist – it was indeed so uplifting and one which we experienced as we journeyed right across India. Simplicity reigned! The engaging smiles of the children with their pearly white teeth, and their willingness to undertake the smallest task, is something which I personally will never forget. The people were just so lovely, friendly and spontaneous. It was such a pleasure to experience their simple way of life, and at various times during our travels, their hospitality. Unfortunately, I believe that nowadays in the more wealthy areas, Western influences are changing the boundaries.

The next day, Andy and Geri joined us and we climbed aboard a train, which incidentally, had many forms of livestock which were also accompanying their owners on the long 18-hour trip, taking us across and down towards the south. One which I know Andy will never choose to take again! That said of course, I personally am pleased that I experienced the true realities of life within India at that time.

It was a vast expanse of arid land, mile after mile of dried-up soil with little evidence of life. Occasionally however, as the train stopped for passengers to be picked up or to depart, there were at the sides of the track people selling their fruits, vegetables, curries etc., pastries, and you found yourself wondering where on earth they had come from, having seen only minimal signs of life as we ventured across.

There was one specific time when the train grounded to a halt and Andy and his friend had alighted to have a cigarette (which incidentally he has for a long time now given up), then found themselves having to scramble back on the train when the driver suddenly decided he was carrying on! No rhyme or reason to the timetable! Their expressions however were hilarious as they ran and jumped aboard as it was gaining speed. A memory which brings a smile to my face when I recall it.

Although we were supposedly in the 1st class area, we were in fact sharing the carriage with the livestock. So funny when you look back on it! The sleeping berths were also shared. There are no words to describe Andy's bemused look. I don't think personally he was at all happy!

The following day we were all told to alight from the train and that a coach would be collecting us. Well, there we all were in the middle of this arid and dusty land praying that we would have transport. Imagine! Eventually an old rickety coach appeared and we were on our way yet again, including the livestock! The journey was indeed very hair-raising to say the least, and we saw many incidents as we proceeded on our journey on tracks mainly filled with potholes., eventually arriving at our destination. Andy and everyone looking incredibly relieved!

After booking into our very meagre hotel, no such luxuries as curtains etc, and after unpacking and changing, we all decided to walk across to the entrance of the Ashram. It had indeed changed a lot since Andy's previous visit. The words to describe it would be 'stunningly beautiful' – we all stood and marvelled at the beauty of the Ashram and were very happy that we had made the journey there. The building was adorned with bright oranges and lemons with gold. The peace engulfed us all.

The men proceeded to sit cross-legged on the left side, whilst the ladies were ushered to the right. Geri and I sat eagerly awaiting Sathya Sai Baba's entrance for Darshan at 3pm. Then we all began to feel this phenomenal amount of energy around our being – it just got stronger and stronger and stronger, then realising that this in fact was emanating from Sathya Sai Baba himself, as he entered the Ashram. We became in total awe of him as he walked down the pathway towards us and through the Ashram.

Andy was now looking far more relaxed and was overjoyed to be in the presence of Sathya Sai Baba, his teacher, whom he had put his total trust in and life from a very young age. He sat watching as his teacher wandered through his flock of devotees, blessing them, talking to various people and encouraging them. This was to be an unforgettable experience and one which we talk about still.

Geri and I used to attend the 4am Darshan, which proved to be a bit of a struggle to get up for in the beginning but soon we became accustomed to this way of life.

I would like to share with you an experience which has remained with me since. A mother and daughter were standing together in the queue to enter early one morning. They had done so for a number of years before, as once a year they would make the long journey right across India to see Sathya Sai Baba. The daughter had been blind since a very young age, and gradually her sight was being restored each year. The mother had been told that they must make this commitment, and that by the time she reached 18 her sight would be fully restored. It was her karma in this life to learn 'appreciation'. She was then 14 years of age and could now make out shapes of people and identify them, and also colours were returning, and she was very excited to tell Sathya Sai Baba.

We experienced many more healings being given, and realised how important it was for Andy to acknowledge the gift which he had been given to carry out the work which his Teacher had bestowed upon him from such an early age.

Chapter 23
Sharing beautiful experiences
we all had together!

(a)

Late one afternoon, we decided to walk to what is known as the Museum, as we were very intrigued as to what we might find here. Upon entering, it was almost magical. The ceiling was very high and shaped as an umbrella, in all various rainbow colours and shining brightly as we began to walk around. There were beautiful inscriptions placed at various displays which were telling the story of each section, dates, years and religion. We soon came to realise that it portrayed the fact that "all Religions are one" – under one umbrella, all believing in the one unity of being – it did not matter whether we were of the Jewish faith, Christian, Buddhist, Jehovah, Mormon, Muslim, etc, we all believed in the one ultimate being, whichever faith we perceive ourselves to be or not, making one realise that when man opens up his mind to these facts then peace can reign for our children, their children and further generations.

The colours were those of the rainbow. The displays themselves were delicately placed, made up of beautiful materials which had all been hand-sewn and were simply stunning. Sathya Sai Baba certainly allowed us all to see the whole picture and instead of dividing our beliefs, we energised our being to that of one – then peace will reign! Instead of man feeling the need to make war with others and use religion as the key to these events to further their own egos and self-importance, as has been the case for many decades to date.

I personally was overwhelmed, having believed from a very young age that all religions are one, and that they are shaped together as an umbrella, and would quote this to others. It used to make me very sad that adults put up such barriers where none needed to exist. For me personally, it was a special interlude and one which I shall never forget.

There were various sayings placed around the museum to inspire and remind people about their own life here on earth, and beautiful writings from the past.

We then all met, and decided to walk to the hillside where there is a beautiful tree which stands overlooking the area and beyond. The view was intriguing, showing the true beauty of the Ashram and beyond. When Sathya Sai Baba was young, he would play there with his friends, and he often produced fruit from the tree and placed it in their hands to eat, which pleased his siblings and you can imagine all the fun they must have had. Sai Baba was aware that he was very different from a very young age, as he was able to materialise objects and his peers were not. When we had seen him in the Ashram he materialised various objects and placed them into his follower's hands.

These days the tree is covered in messages which have been written and tied on with ribbon in remembrance of those who have passed over. It was amazingly calm and peaceful there as we all watched the evening sunset disappearing into the darkness!

(b)

Late one afternoon, Geri and I were sitting talking to a shopkeeper and his family, who sold the most amazing materials which came from Misor. It is renowned throughout the world for the most beautiful hand-woven cloths etc, the colours being magnificent with amazing designs. Suddenly his brother called out that Sathya Sai Baba was being driven slowly down the road, having visited his elephant, which he did at the same time every day. Now this road was like a dirt track full of mighty potholes and moving mud as the rainy season had just finished, and there was a cart being pulled by oxen. Cows, chickens, geese etc scattered anywhere and everywhere. You had to experience it to believe it!

The car approached very slowly indeed, and as I was standing literally in front the shop, it stopped for a few minutes right in front of me. Sathya Sai Baba raised his hand and smiled at me, and in that instant I had a truly amazing experience. His eyes glowed in love and kindness towards me, and I knew immediately that he knew every single thing about me and my life. I can only describe my feelings – it was as though I had no earthly body, it just didn't exist, and I was floating gently in front of him. The peace and love which surrounded my being was truly amazing, and one which I shall never ever forget and cherish to this day. It changed my life, as I too now had experienced the awesome presence Sathya Sai Baba myself.

(c)

The shopkeeper who had befriended us all over a period of

61

time, and where Andy chose beautiful cloths to have made into various items of clothing for both himself and Geri, invited our group to go to his home and receive his hospitality. The family made us all very welcome and we all sat and chatted and sang Bhajans and Andy played a guitar, together with the other men.

They passed round to us a piece of cake, but we noticed that they did not have any – we later found out that he had spent his meagre takings on us and there was not enough to go round for his family. An amazing gesture of kindness, and it was truly humbling. It had been given in love – there are many lessons we can learn from these people. I personally never ever take an act of kindness for granted, I receive it always in love. Especially, when you think that they have little but wish to share with others. They just simply live by pure standards, they are not greedy, they do not need to impress anyone – they give from their heart. They are the ones who are truly living life!

Again, there was another occasion when Andy, Geri and 2 more members of the group and I decided to go by car to a monument which Andy had been told to visit by an Indian gentleman who had befriended him, which was a few miles away. Well, this was going to prove the worst driving nightmare we could have encountered. Literally nerve wracking! Certainly not for the faint-hearted.

We arrived at a very small village which was extremely quiet and very, very hot, and there were just a few chickens wandering around, and then we were shown into a small shrine where it is said that Jesus walked, and there are small footprints in the ground which it is believed are his, when he spent time in India preaching his divine word. All those centuries ago! It certainly made quite an impact on us all. Again, the peace was amazing.

(d)

There were other times when we would meet up in a small café which looked more like a tent, with pieces of material hung around and chairs scattered about, where we would discuss our experiences and plans to date and catch up on our thoughts for the day.

We came into contact with many nationalities from all around the world who had travelled the globe to experience the teachings of Sathya Sai Baba, as we indeed had done. You can imagine all the interesting conversations which took place during our stay here, learning about others' experiences and cultures, and also their ways of life. Everyone participated in the ambience of the whole experience, and I am sure it had a great impact on their lives too, seeing all the different nationalities from around the world, mixing together and exchanging experiences, using their hands to demonstrate and express to those who could not speak their language what exactly they were trying to say, and the laughter was so infectious!

(e)

One specific incident which weighed heavily on Andy's heart involved a young boy whom he discovered very late one evening sleeping in a sack outside his door. It was around 4am and Andy had wanted to see the early sunrise. Andy immediately recognised him as a young lad who did loads of heavy lifting of client's baggage, and ran all the errands which were imposed upon him by the hotel and guests. He always seemed to be working so hard. He was extremely thin and undernourished, but had the most beautiful smile! Andy was keen to learn more about him, so he decided to talk with him.

This young lad told him that he was the breadwinner for his large family. He would therefore on his day off walk 12 long miles to his home and hand over his meagre wages to his parents. He would rest and then start walking back at around 2am the next morning to start his shift again. There were only three hours in each day for him to get some sleep, as his jobs were many, and he was on call to clients. Then he would climb into the sack and sleep wherever he could find and then his day would start all over again.

He would knock on the door to see if Geri and I needed any assistance in any way, and one morning I was using a mini iron to press some form of clothing, (which I cannot remember). He was standing looking at me with an expression of fear in his eyes, I could not believe it! He had never seen an iron and for some reason thought it was an evil instrument. After some encouragement by me, he watched, suddenly realising this object pressed clothes (something which we in the Western world take for granted). Immediately he stated that his mother would be overjoyed to have one of these. So yes, you can guess, the iron travelled to his home for his mother, for when the electricity was put on.

Andy told us all about his predicament, so we all decided that we should club together and give him clothes etc for himself and his family members. Money also changed hands, so that when he arrived home his mother could put it towards the electricity as his mother could not afford to use it. Imagine! They were living in very meagre circumstances.

Then, when it came to the weekend, Andy had arranged that his brother would come and collect him, and together they would take a bus back with all the relevant parcels for their family and others in the village. It was the custom that if you were fortunate to receive food or anything, when you had taken a share, you would then pass to others.

Andy was saddened by this family's situation. This is a side to Andy which not many see; his ability to see the wider picture and help whenever he possibly can. His generosity is given from the heart and is second to none. He believes totally in giving to the less fortunate when the need arises and circumstances present themselves to him. He does it with reverence.

Chapter 24

Summary of our time spent

Summing up, the time which we spent all together with Andy and Geri at the Ashram, in his own words, was "as close to a Garden of Eden as one can get – energising – a magnetic and blissful location". It is a very simple and peaceful way of life. Certainly not filled with egotistical and greedy human beings who are forever striving for more money, more status, more materialistic items than others, all their lives – such a sad state of affairs! Instead, it is a more loving, kind, caring attitude to their fellow men and women, and they opened up their hearts and homes to all of us. Food and drink was offered freely, even though we realised that in some cases they could ill afford to do so – to me personally this meant a lot. The true meaning of friendship, giving all to others. Very humbling, and we experienced this on a lot of occasions.

You can imagine how we all felt when it was time for us to depart, and leave these beautiful families and their simple ways of living life. In Andy's brother's case he actually decided to postpone his flight and stayed there for a further six months to study and learn more of Sathya Sai Baba's teachings.

Andy, Geri and all of us realised what an amazing and diverse journey we had been on, and our experiences shared together, and how blessed we all were to have had the opportunity at first hand to experience India without the frills.

Unfortunately today the Western world will have influenced the simplicity of some areas to the detriment of the people, but in hindsight we are all very grateful to have gained knowledge of how life existed for all previous generations to that point in time, and I feel we will always be extremely grateful to Andy for letting us join him on one of his amazing journeys to India.

However, once we returned to Mumbai Station reality soon kicked in. We encountered a UK tourist on one of the original mobiles, talking so loudly, obviously full of his own importance, striding about the platform, and the local people were in disbelief, as I must say we were too. Such arrogance! It made all of us cringe, to say the least.

Chapter 25

Andy – Truly amazing!

No one can doubt his worth, and certainly not I, who personally have seen his expertise with my own eyes – people recovering from very, very serious health issues, totally restored by Andy's healing.

Visitations

One visitation was where Sathya Sai Baba appeared one night in Andy's doorway – the force threw him out of his bed. The voice said:

> **"I am the stem of the flower**
> **You are my petals**
> **I give you strength to cling to me and**
> **flourish in all beauty**
> **Take the water from the stem**
> **The water is my love**
> **Call upon me and I shall guide**
> **And protect you always"**

Very profound! He who guides him each step of the way, so that he in turn can then help as many people as possible through the power of unconditional love.

Another of Andy's treasured sayings of Sathya Sai Baba is the following:

"If you help just one person in need, this act becomes holier than a church filled with a thousand people"

Having read about many topics on various religions and philosophies, Andy feels in his own personal opinion that many religions are structured to believe that theirs is the right way, which as a large number of us have come to believe, is not the case!

Using Your Imagination

The easiest way to understand this symbolically is to imagine a diamond in the sky. The diamond has many facets and from each facet, if there is light coming from behind it comes as a ray of light. Each religion is connecting to its one individual facet. They can't see the other facets and consequently they're not seeing the oneness – the omnipresent force of the universe. They are all connected to exactly the same source, at the end of the day.

Another time, Andy had a vision in which he saw a life-sized statue of his spiritual guru. Then lo and behold, one of his patients, a gentleman whom he was treating for leukemia, and who was incidentally cured by Andy's treatment, gave him a life-sized statue of Sathya Sai Baba – in stunning saffron robes - which now stands sedately radiating his presence in the Healing Sanctuary on entry. Amazing, a piece of sculpture which he commissioned his girlfriend, who is a sculptor, to do. Also, a further two pieces of sculpture in Sathya Sai Baba's image were added at a later date.

Andy genuinely believes Sathya Sai Baba is his protector, his guardian angel, keeping him steadfast on his pathway. I totally agree!

Chapter 26

Traumatic experiences

Here are three examples of where situations occurred where Andy was saved from trauma.

(1)

The first one was in a dream state, when he was entering his front door as a vehicle drew up outside. It was an orange Transit van with the words "Sai Baba Auto Repairs" on the side. Andy walked back down the pathway, and there he was in the driving seat and winding down the window, beaming at him. Then the window went back up and he drove off.

Next morning, Andy was worrying about going out because of this dream. Whilst driving along the motorway on the outside lane at full speed, he found himself to have no brakes whatsoever! The master cylinder had failed. He managed to gradually slow down by continually pumping the brakes and gradually drove back home which was not far away.

He was extremely shaken up by the experience and decided to call a car repairer. Yes, he arrived in a bright orange transit! On the side it had written 'Stephen Brown Auto Repairs. S.B. for Sai Baba!

(2)

On the second occasion, he was driving over what is known

as the Cobden Bridge area of Bitterne, Southampton, when he came to traffic lights which were due to turn green. Then a loud voice told him to 'slow down' twice. Which incidentally he did, when all of a sudden, a red Porsche suddenly emerged, racing down the road. Unbelievable! It had in fact jumped the lights. If Andy had not slowed right down, the vehicle would have collided with him, and the consequences would have been dire.

(3)

On a third occasion, Andy awoke and was aware of yet another vision where two cars were involved. This made him feel very uneasy indeed. He decided to put off travelling until later in the day when the traffic would have subsided quite a bit. He was feeling hesitant, naturally. He made his way towards Ocean Village, where he again was sitting at traffic lights on red. He was unaware of any vehicles behind him, having checked his mirror constantly, when upon another glance he could see a vehicle approaching at high speed. The vehicle hit Andy's Mini and in these moments he called out to Sai Baba to help him.

When alighting from his car he could see that the Cavalier car was badly damaged. The driver had a look of astonishment upon his face, whilst staring at the wheel of the Mini – it was completely intact, no damage whatsoever! His call for help had indeed been heard.

At this moment in time, Andy was fully aware of how the predictions were now unfolding and he was able to use his 'healing' gift to help others – his prime purpose in life!

"To serve others in their hour of need"

Chapter 27

Malcolm – Andy's father

I should like to relate now one of Andy's proudest moments in his life, which occurred when his father Malcolm McKellar became very ill after suffering a stroke, followed by a heart attack. It left him feeling very debilitated. He was unable to walk any distance, just a few yards. He had quite a collection of various pills and potions which he was constantly taking.

This was the man who had continually caused great suffering, hurt and humiliation to Andy as a child, and who had discredited his abilities and knowledge of all spiritual matters throughout his life. Andy decided to approach him and offered to give him a series of healing sessions. After due consideration, he decided to accept this offer.

What an amazing string of events. Unbelievable! At last the tide began to turn. The healing began to have a profound effect on his father, and he went from strength to strength. His father in his own words said, "Andrew I was your father once; now you're mine". Malcolm also asked his son how much longer he had to live, and he replied that it would be a few more years yet providing he stopped smoking altogether, which was possibly responsible for his previous major health problems.

Then, totally unexpectedly, his father decided to part with his mother and return to where he had been born, namely Camden Town in London. His parents however would remain bonded until his passing a number of years later.

Malcolm maintained his contact with his son, and sent patients to Andy on a regular basis. He was extremely happy to be back in his son's life and immensely proud of his son's achievements. At last the rifts were finally healed between them both.

Chapter 28

Awareness in association with his spiritual helpers

Andy's awareness of his spiritual helpers grew and grew, and he felt safe in the knowledge he was not alone. During such a time Andy became very aware of a doctor's presence and he was in fact assisting him. He had a wide knowledge of various illnesses and is a great help to this day. His name is Doctor Williams (DFC). Only Andy sensed his presence. However, one night whilst Andy was lying on his bed a truly remarkable occurrence took place.

Doctor Williams appeared at the end of his bed, a well-dressed gentleman wearing a full-length cape and a low top hat, from his appearance obviously from the Victorian era. He decided to walk down the side of the bed, and Andy became uncomfortable and hid under the covers. When he opened his eyes, the doctor had gone. Over the years he has become a great helper to Andy and some of his patients have seen his presence.

Moving on now to about five years later, Andy became aware of yet another spirit doctor, Doctor Cotton. Andy was convinced he had shared another lifetime with him, in yet another 'out of body experience'. His specialty was tumours.

Andy is associated also with having great respect for North American Indians who guide him through his pathway of life.

One of his favourite stories is about a young girl whose name was Linda Martel. She passed away due to kidney failure at the age of five in the Channel Islands, the year before Andy was born. She had been born with spina bifida in 1961 but she had a remarkable gift of healing from a very young age, sitting in her pram, through touch.

Andy decided to make contact with her mother to let her know how impressed he was by her daughter's dedication as a young child to helping others. In turn, he received a photograph of Linda with her mother.

A while later patients informed him that they had seen a little girl who would often come and sit on their laps. Then Linda appeared to Andy. Yes – this was the little girl who appeared in the picture and whom Andy was fully aware of. She too gives a hand when needed. Remarkable!

Chapter 29

Gaining knowledge and healing techniques to promote 'wellness' in others

One day he was approached by a nurse in relation to a patient of hers who was suffering from leukaemia. Her name was Anne. This lady was a widow in her fifties and she was extremely ill. Accompanying this, she was also clinically depressed and mentally unstable, living in fear of the unknown and trusting no one. Anne was also very weak and lethargic. Very sad.

However, the nurse persuaded her to visit Andy's healing sanctuary for about two months, saying she would accompany her. Eventually she gained strength and vitality and had her life back. She was also spreading the word of Andy's incredible healing work and how she had great faith in him. She had trust and confidence in his abilities, and therefore began gaining trust in others again. Remarkable, when you think of it.

Then disaster struck, by means of a very bad storm, and Anne got soaking wet, which unfortunately led her down a spiral of ill health yet again. Sometimes, no matter how hard Andy tries to help save someone, when their time is nigh on this earthly plane there is nothing he can do. Anne had now resigned herself to being in her home.

One evening, he received a call yet again from the nurse requesting him to make a visit up north to her home, having no indication whatsoever that Anne was in the background listening.

78

With Geri accompanying him on this long trip, they arrived fairly late in the evening and he found himself driving through elegant gates onto a long drive which took him towards what looked like a stately residence. On arriving they were directed by a maid to go up the wooden staircase to Anne's bedroom.

Andy was very distraught to see the deterioration in Anne, but realised his healing would provide peace and tranquillity for her and assist in her passing over to the other side, giving her great assurance. Andy was very saddened by this state of events but knew it was totally out of his hands, as it was Anne's 'time'. He kissed her gently on the forehead, knowing that it was the last time on this earth he would see her.

Then a few months later, Andy found himself yet again travelling 'out of body' and at very high speed. He found himself outside Anne's oak front door. On entering, he climbed up the familiar spiral staircase to Anne's bedroom door. He had three attempts at walking through the door, and once inside there was Anne looking extremely angry and stressed alone on the bed. She had been unable to accept that she was in fact dead.

"What are you doing here? Why hasn't anybody come for me?" she said. All of a sudden Andy realised why all these events had occurred, and that in fact Anne had suffered extreme isolation and fear, and trusted no one. This was how the present situation had occurred. She now felt stranded and in an extremely agitated state of mind.

Andy was quick to respond. "Anne, no one has come to see you because you have died". Her reply was "Don't talk so stupid".

She responded by pinching her arms and then remarking that she could feel herself, believing very pointedly she was alive! She stated suddenly, that she was "not going with them". Andy could not see anything as she pointed to the wall. However, then he noted small flickers of light which then exploded in a swirling mass of white light.

Anne had become very trusting of Andy in her last days. Andy was aware of her face changing and all the sadness and anxiety leaving her body, being replaced with calmness as she gained clarity of mind. She turned and quietly and reverently walked into the tunnel without looking back, no words being exchanged at all. Anne had been fully aware that Andy had always had her best interests at heart – solace had now entered her being.

Andy will forever be grateful that he was able to help Anne whilst here on earth and in opening up the entrance to her life beyond the veil. His dedication to his patients is simply amazing, and this is a truly remarkable example of his dedication to mankind and to serving his fellow men and woman, children and animals alike, in the words of Sathya Sai Baba.

Chapter 30

Love All, Serve All

These are prominent words which Andy adheres to daily, and which all of us in our own specific ways can do in our everyday lives whether it be large or small.

An act of kindness and love for our fellow men is *"What is so important"* and so in our daily lives remember to spread the love. The more we do, the less negativity is able to surface and we can bring a new chapter into our lives and those of our families and all children, grandchildren and future generations. Let's follow Andy's example and be 'positive' – he is!

I would like to mention also that I too try to adhere to this motto daily.

Chapter 31

A Vision of Jesus:
very profound words indeed

Jesus told him "Andy, you don't need to baptise people with water – you baptise them with love".

Chapter 32

A more positive phase in life

In 1997 Andy received a telephone call from a lady whose name was Geri who wished to know whether he would be willing to give a talk on his experiences of healing etc. This he agreed, and upon meeting her he realised that this beautiful lady would indeed in time agree to marry him. This is where I met Andy.

A year later, they were married at a lovely hotel in the New Forest which had amazing gardens. It was a very colourful day as the men were in Indian dress and the women were dressed in saris. The bride looking stunning. It was such a joyous occasion with family and friends too – a complete cross-section of people too.

Geri's pretty little daughter Kristie Anne was in attendance by her side. Geri is in fact a very gifted medium in her own right, and told Andy that in the future he would be treating many cancer patients. This has become a reality. They also believed that they had spent a previous life experience together.

Geri herself has been studying the Buddhist pathway for many years, and is very knowledgeable on the subject. They indeed complimented each other with their skills.

They started their married life together, renting a small house in Southampton. One evening they became aware of a tiny ball of light in the kitchen doorway. They both saw it disperse and suddenly they were aware of the presence of an old lady with white hair and a thick knitted shawl who had joined them in the room; she could only move with a stick. Then gradually she began fading away.

In time, an elderly gentleman came to see Andy who had arthritic hips, and he began to tell him that in the past he too had lived in the house. He had actually been born there, and so with this knowledge Andy divulged the information about the lady he had seen and immediately he responded. It was in fact the next-door neighbour, whose name was Beatrice. She had always stood at the gate, obviously people watching.

One day, Andy saw that a house had come onto the market opposite and after a discussion with Geri they proceeded to go ahead and purchase it. The house itself had already appeared to Andy in a dream, with a beautiful garden. However, they were unaware of the spiritual occupancy it came with. They were to have many experiences to deal with over time. Children's voices, laughter, exuberance of youngsters running up and down the stairs, but no sightings as such – it must have had quite an adverse effect on their health.

Over time it became evident that Andy needed to have more space in which to see his clients and provide for their comfort. So within the year they found suitable premises with an annexe, which was to be the ideal solution at that time.

It was their first sanctuary, and they were thrilled. In Andy's words, it was 'absolutely beautiful'.

Around this time, Andy received the news that his father had been taken sick again (having ignored Andy's advice not to smoke). He did undergo a heart bypass operation. The doctor remarked how well he was doing, but it was short lived. He had a massive stroke during this time. They were both very saddened by the news and to see the deterioration in him, and realised that in fact his days were numbered.

During this time, Geri heard a very persistent voice with a Scottish accent and saw a petite lady with masses of black hair. She said, 'My name's Annie and I've come to take ma laddie'. No one could recall the name. However, Andy remembered that his father had two sisters, Betty and Helen – their parents had parted when they were young, and their mother remained in the UK with Andrew's father, who never mentioned her to Andy as he was growing up. His father had only been reunited with them in the past three years prior to his death.

Andy felt that he needed to make contact to see how events were unfolding. The sisters were shocked at hearing the description of Annie Brown, as they had been trying to locate her for some time. The description fitted their mother.

Chapter 33

A new turn of events

Thankfully, Andy's work was evolving at a very hectic pace and it was obvious to him and Geri that they needed to up sticks and move again. Demand was increasing, as his abilities were increasingly being used in many more fields of illness. Amazing!

Having realised the necessity for client parking facilities and easy access for the disabled patients, they decided to look further out on the outskirts of Southampton, and were recommended a village called Burridge which was not far from the M27 motorway, local train route and Whiteley Shopping Centre. Also appealing was the fact that it wasn't far from the countryside. There were also amenities in Locksheath, which was a only a short distance away by car.

They investigated the possibility and came across the dream home as it had appeared to Geri in a dream, and were both delighted as they wished to bring up their children in a lovely environment. It was an American chalet-style bungalow. When looking down from the road you could see a half moon driveway, so this would prove to be ideal for patients driving in and parking their vehicles. Also, it was an ideal location for the new Healing Sanctuary.

One of Andy's patients thought it would be a great idea to publicise his arrival in the area in a local paper, and to let people know that he would be operating from his own Sanctuary –

heading the article up "World Famous Healer Moves to Burridge'. The lady in question stated that she had been very sceptical at first hand of Andy's abilities, but after investigation she now had the highest regard for him, stating "He is indeed a tremendous asset to the people of Burridge".

Their happiness unfortunately was to be short lived and they were totally unprepared for this. It was an incident which just snowballed out of control. They realised that the new neighbour had a vile attitude towards Andy's vocation, and it turned very quickly into a campaign by this man to make their lives unbearable, to say the least. A nightmare for them and the children was unfolding.

A few days later as Andy was getting out of his car, a voice from next door shouted "a privilege to have you in the street is it! We'll see about that, won't we?" He did everything in his power to make their lives as unpleasant as possible, and then began campaigning and bringing in other neighbours to join his side, managing to persuade them to write letters of complaint to the council and exaggerating the circumstances of his clients using his driveway. The accusations went on and on and on, and eventually Andy even started receiving Enforcement Notices. These were in relation to getting the Healing Sanctuary closed down.

It never made sense, as there were other businesses being operated from people's homes in the road, including all types of lorries, 4 x 4s etc using it which caused far more damage, and can still be seen to this day, but of course these were never mentioned at the time and never brought to the Council's notice.

Personally, I believe his neighbour was of a particular religion and his ignorance in regard to Andy's gift of healing was obvious. Some of the neighbours were even distributing leaflets warning others that Andy was living in the road. So very, very bizarre! Then they stated that his clients could run over their children in the road, completely oblivious of their own misgivings! This was a wide road and the houses had huge gardens where children would play. It was not the sort of area where children played in the street in any case.

The Council was extremely negative towards Andy. It clearly was a case of sheep following sheep. Geri had never experienced this type of behaviour before, and it all began to affect her health. This was a young woman in her 30s who became terrified to even leave her home and walk down the lane to the post box to send letters.

I know this is 100% true, as I too became a target of this abuse. After spending the evening quietly meditating in the back garden with Geri and watching the sun go down, I had decided to go home when we were greeted by appalling behaviour. (In my mind however, it was obvious that it was they who were being abusive and vitriolic to Andy and Geri, and not the other way round). Geri is a very softly-spoken, sophisticated young woman and certainly is not in the habit of using this type of language, let alone abusive behaviour. To this day she conducts herself in a very graceful manner, following her Buddhist pathway very seriously, and her conduct is exemplary.

It was also apparent that the objectors had not even met Andy or his lovely family on a personal level but had taken the word of others to try and destroy his livelihood and stop him helping others, which he has dedicated his life to for many years and is still doing.

After this event, within the next few days Geri collapsed and was hospitalised. She was placed in intensive care, and it was declared that she had a suspected bleed on her brain caused by all the stress and worry which she had undergone since moving into this road. Geri has never fully recovered.

There was a case brought against Andy, and regardless of all the poetic prose which were sent in, it proved irrelevant to their cause and Andy won his case. He had his hours reduced along with the number of clients he could see each day. Andy decided to take his case to the Secretary of State. His representative felt that Andy could see more patients and work between the hours of 9 am to 5 pm, Monday to Friday. Common sense prevailing at last. I think it's called 'poetic justice'.

After a while, as Geri was regaining her health, it was decided that they would move, and they began looking for a desirable property where they would be able to add a Healing Sanctuary for Andy. They found their present home in Locksheath, where Andy currently operates from and which has worked extremely well for many years. It is in Locks Road and very easy to find. There is parking outside. It is a quiet area and trouble free, with easy access for patients coming from the M27 motorway.

It is also interesting to note that over the years Andy has been able to use his healing skills and help neighbours in the surrounding area, and still does to this day.

Chapter 34

From my perspective

I would like to convey to you with their permission and share with you all my belief that in a family environment where their father is constantly in demand his family have coped extremely well, as it could not have been an easy pathway for them having to forego his presence at various activities during their lives. Geri, however, has always been extremely supportive and in return acknowledged Andy's dedication to his work and is very proud of his achievements in helping others.

Chapter 35
Sarah and Andrew Jnr

Sarah and Andrew Jnr are Andrew's two children from his first marriage. Andrew says, "They mean so much to me and we have stayed together throughout the years. They are two amazing people and I am very proud of both of them. They are not just my children, they are my friends. Love you both".

Chapter 36

Marcus

A few years ago Andy heard his spiritual teacher Sathya Sai Baba telepathically say to him:

"Once the baby leaves the darkness of the womb it shall recognise its mother. The baby, while in the womb where it is dark, is encompassed in protection. Once brought into the light of day, there is an instant recognition of the mother. The baby does not understand or know the mother. The instant recognition causes the baby to trust implicitly.

"So when man awakens from his long sleep and frees himself from the dark womb of constant material thought, he shall grow, develop and learn much about himself. And like the baby, shall receive the mother's full attention and love, protection and guidance.

"Yes, once man awakens to spiritual truth, his true mother of life shall guide him to the kingdom of love and light".

Before he was born, Geri and Andy were in America, staying at a hotel in Tampa when she had a profound experience and one which would change their lives, which she was at the time unable to explain. She saw a spirit form come towards her out of the bedroom wall – the lady was carrying a young baby in her arms and holding out the child to Geri.

At the same time as this occurred, outside of the main building on a pain of glass there was an amazing portrait of the Virgin

Mary, which had appeared from nowhere, and the day before had not existed. It was drawing crowds of people and was to become a phenomenon in Tampa until very recently, when the glass was shattered. People travelled from all over the globe to experience the happening for themselves. It was truly beautiful.

When Geri returned home it was confirmed that she was in fact carrying a baby. She also had another vision from her spirit guide Lanto, who told her that the baby should be treasured "*because in fact he was in a past life a Lama from Tibet – a holy being*".

Following suit, Andy had a sudden out-o- body experience. He watched as a doctor came towards him carrying a young baby and placed it in his arms. Andy was surprised at how long the baby was, and his attention was drawn to a distinctive mark just above the baby's top lip. The doctor told him, "*This child is coming to you, look after him. He was a Lama of the Highest Order. He will do much good in the world*".

As a young baby Marcus looked the image of a Buddha. His features were far older in a beautiful, peaceful calming way and he held his head in a regal pose – looking very eloquent and having great awareness for one so young. Unique, in his own right. His body was long and the birthmark was there just above his lip as predicted.

When Andy showed his photograph to one of his Indian acquaintances, who incidentally was a former interpreter for the Tibetan Dalai Lama himself, he just kept saying "*Lama, Lama, Lama*".

Marcus's first spoken words were *Swami, Swami* – not mummy or daddy – which in Indian means Guru. Fascinating but true! He was two years of age at the time.

His demeanour is that of his mother Geri. He has a quiet, unassuming and gentle personality. Very caring of others.

As he grew he became fascinated as he watched his mother meditate and would compose himself and sit by her side from a very young age, with a knowingness beyond his years.

Marcus is now a very honourable young man and follows in his father's footsteps and has the same healing qualities, and in the future I am sure will be assisting him. He has incredible psychic abilities too.

He is now attending college and in his spare time concentrating on Kirlian Photography, where the camera is capable of taking a picture of the aura surrounding a person. Marcus has his own specialised equipment for doing this. It is fascinating to see the picture taken and how all the colours of energy in your aura actually portray your characteristics at that specific time. Marcus then follows this by giving an in-depth reading to each client about the contents within the picture.

It is a very interesting phenomenon. I enjoyed my visit to have a photograph taken recently and insight from the reading of my own aura, and was amazed at the colours surrounding my body. You should try it some time! Marcus is operating from his parents' home.

We all have our gifts, but sometimes we feel inadequate to pursue them. Therefore, in my mind it is great to see Marcus moving forward on his pathway with great positivity in working towards helping others. Easier said than done. I know!

Marcus and his father have become closer now and share quality time together. There is great banter between them. I am sure that Marcus will be accomplishing great things as he matures into manhood. He is a credit to his parents.

Certainly a young man to be proud of, his moral attitude towards his fellow man is admirable. Refreshing in this day and age, I am sure you will agree!

Chapter 37

Kristie Anne

Kristie Anne is a stunning young lady who has great work ethics, and achieved beyond all expectations in her working environment and has recently moved into a beautiful home with her partner. She has met her 'Knight in Shining Armour' so to speak and is looking forward to sharing with Mark their future pathway!

They enjoy going travelling and so far have been to some amazing places throughout the globe, also setting themselves up to take part in various challenges far and near in aid of different charities. Admirable!

It is refreshing following the posts, and seeing also the great love and respect which shows in their faces. "True Love".

Indeed, a daughter to be proud of!

Chapter 38

How healing works throughout the body;
Chakra Chart and examples

Andy would describe his gift as being passed through his hands from a higher source which he himself believes in totally.

We are, as we all know, living in a very sceptical era. Man can at times have a very negative attitude, especially when he is unable to see the 'whys' and 'wherefores' of how it all works, and indeed cannot fathom out the unexplainable.

Here is an attempt to analyse it in simple form.

Our systems run through various stages of energy, and at birth these colours are in balance. These are called chakra points (see illustration overleaf), from the base of the spine, up through various points in our body to the top of our heads. Each point has its own individual colour, as you can see from the drawing.

At birth they are perfectly attuned, rather like a new car, but as time passes the parts become worn and sluggish. As we are all aware in these modern times, it becomes more and more difficult to function and eventually our bodies too begin to struggle and we feel less energetic, more lethargic and unable to concentrate, and we find ourselves on a downward spiral as our energy depletes.

In some cases also, we are in discomfort and pain and our colour energy has dissolved, leaving us with only the option (so we believe), of going to see our GP to discuss our health issues.

At this point in time, if we have no medical answers to our illness, then we start to seek others. As we remain 'off colour', so to speak, the term often used and which of course now we are aware and begin to understand how this saying has come about.

From Andy's perception, it is very obvious what is happening to us from birth and the reasons for our decline. The colours need to be energised therefore by a healer who understands exactly what is happening to us, and therefore can assist us in getting back on track, so to speak.

CHAKRA POINTS

Base of spine	Red	Throat area	Blue
Just below navel	Orange	Heart region	Green
Solar plexus	Yellow	In between eyes	Indigo
Very top of head	Violet		

As you will see, the heart chakra is notably the heart engine, the emotional side of our personality. Then the throat chakra which is where our communication skills come into place, and so on... Allow the colour in one or more of those regions to fade or badly distort and you will find yourself with positive energy literally mutating into negative energy.

Andy's healing sanctuary is very calming, bright and private. Music is softly playing in the background. There is a very cosy, loving atmosphere, especially when the log burner is lit.

When Andy receives a new patient into his healing sanctuary, he likes to make them feel comfortable in his presence. Andy ensures that there are no uneasy moments as they state their medical problems and how they expect he may be able to assist.

Then the patient sits on a low stool which enables Andy to move to where he believes the point is to start his healing. At this time Andy will have assessed the body as a whole, and looking to see (as he calls it), a greenish mist covering the problem areas of the body. Green is his tool. It does not diagnose the problem, however.

Then he will attune into the high energy level and within a short time he is aware of it passing through him in the form of heat through his hands.

During this time he involves his spiritual helpers, such as Dr. Cotton, who helps with tumours and the like, and Dr. Williams, who can help with a whole range of illnesses, due to both their vast knowledge and experience in helping others.

Andy will then place his hands on the patient's back, starting at the top of the spinal cord, and working his way down. The patient at this point will indeed feel a surge of tremendous heat passing through from his hands. If you were to put a thermometer here, it will always show a normal reading regardless. Quite bizarre!

Then he will place his hands over their eyes, and sometimes

101

they will see amazing colours. Not all patients do, however. At the first session this may be due to the fact that the patient is suffering with anxiety. It can be a dull and dingy colour, browns, black, greys etc. It confirms to Andy the imbalance within the patient to be pronounced.

We now come to the very interesting part. As the energy begins to work the patient will be strongly aware of the heat, and it is now that this energy is in part restoring the balance. Swelling may start reducing and pain also, and other ailments. The list is endless. In some other cases it will take longer.

In the case of patients suffering with ME, the colour is yellow and in the cases of cancer and tumours it is pink. There are some rare occasions when a patient does not feel anything, this however does not mean that the healing isn't taking place.

This evidence has been divulged by patients and assessed as such. One of these patients was a lady in her mid-60s who was an ME sufferer over a number of years. Upon Andy placing his hands over her eyes, bright yellow of various shades appeared and were there for 10 minutes or so. On one occasion she was released from the flu-like symptoms which she had experienced for a long period, and was ecstatic with the outcome. Pure joy!

Andy recalls vividly seeing the outline of her body in a yellow glow – free of any ME symptoms.

It is hard to put into words how it must have felt for her having suffered for so long from this illness which is simply soul destroying, and then over a short period of time gradually experiencing feeling and energy in her body, and all the symptoms disappearing. She made a full recovery back to good health. Simply fantastic!

Andy emphasises yet again that colour represents energy and in turn 'colour and heat go together'.

Another example

Thinking back in time, there was a patient called Keith who had a number of large tumours on his body and he was indeed in a very bad state. He was absolutely overwhelmed by the situation which he was experiencing and had approached Andy for help. The evening after his healing session, he awoke from sleeping and felt a burning sensation all over his body. The heat was very intense, and he could see various colours of light within the room, which incidentally was dark.

The patient turned on the light, and his wife could see hand prints all over his back in the positions Andy had placed his hands earlier that evening. The tumours had vanished. Every single one. Unbelievable!

We can only imagine the relief his wife would have felt and in turn the patient when the reality sunk in.

Chapter 39

Reincarnation

Another of Andy's strong beliefs lies in the fact of reincarnation from one life to another, whereby in this life we are given opportunities to experience challenges and all aspects of life which we have failed in previously, and faced with yet again in this life time. Andy also believes that the world as such follows a universal karmic pattern, of which we are all a part of and responsible to committing to, during our own life span.

Too deep? Maybe, but in simple terms instead of being and having a negative attitude always and being critical all the time. Think how positively you would come across if you placed yourself in Andy's shoes and gave to others your time, your experiences and your individual skills, and to teach others. We can all sow a seed of hope and love in others, and from this small seed a mighty strength of understanding would be received by others. How much happier you would be!

Food for thought, don't you think?

Chapter 40

Summary of Andy and his open views on life

Andy remains modest in relation to his healing abilities, at times being amazed at how his life has been transformed, and in turn how many people both here in the UK and around the world he has been able to help attain good health over the years and to date. Andy's motto is:

LOVE ALL, SERVE ALL
In the words of Satya Sai Baba

Over the past 30 years plus Andy has taken these words extremely seriously, believing always that a lot of his successes are due to the fact that he refuses to accept that there are some illnesses which are incurable, and therefore he is always very determined to prove this.

Andy believes, however, that throughout history there has been a long record of violence and prejudices which he himself would like to think will change in future generations, and "Love thy neighbour" will be far more appropriate, bringing peace for our offspring and their future generations.

Looking back a few hundred years, there were gifted psychics and healers around who were good, honest, caring and loving people. What did religion do? It drowned them, burned them, judged them as witches and warlocks, not recognising the fact that they were around well before religious faiths were even created.

So, has he been the target of religious prejudice? Yes – The worst 'bible thumping' onslaught came from a lady branding him in a newspaper article as the Devil himself, stating that Jesus Christ was the only person capable of performing miracles, she raged. Christ would be returning soon, she warned, and Andrew should accept that only through Him could he reach God. Jesus died to save us from our sins.

To me personally, this is totally absurd in this day and age, having myself witnessed many miracles as a result of Andy's healing and patients being restored to good health. I have visited India, where thousands of people travelled every year seeking help for themselves and others and were restored back to good health. We cannot judge, as we do not walk in their shoes. We have no right to.

Andy's belief is that **"Love is action"**. Service is **"action"**.

Chapter 41

Mediumship Reading
by
Geri MacKellar

Suffering loss and bereavement is absolutely devastating, life-changing and traumatic. When loved ones are taken suddenly, there are so often many things which have been unsaid: *"If only I had said this"* or *"If only they had said that"*. So many people live with unnecessary guilt after someone has passed to the other side of life. It can be so healing to get a message of comfort from the 'other side'.

Number 1.

Geri:

'Come in Terry'

Terry:

Hi Geri nice to meet you. I'm a bit sceptical but I've heard a lot about your work.

Geri:

No problem Terry. Let's see how we get on. I'm sure it will be fine!

Take a seat. Now as soon as you are sitting down I can see loads of sparkly lights come in and around you, they are now beside me. As the lights shine to your left and behind you that tells me it is in-law side of the family. I have your father-in-law actually, and it's your ex father-in-law Ken here.

Terry:

Yes, my ex father-in-law is Ken. I'm not surprised he is here.

Geri:

He is telling me to tell you to stop feeling Guilty life happens! You couldn't help it.

Terry:

Oh my God I feel emotional, his eyes filled up.

Geri:

You still help your mother-in-law, is her name Jean or Joan?

Terry:

Yes Jean.

Geri:

Life happens Terry. Ken says "He knows it was difficult with his daughter, your ex-wife. Ken says he likes your new lady and thank you for keeping an eye on Jean for him".

Terry:

Wow!! I feel lighter for that. I feel so much guilt as when Ken was dying I was leaving my ex-wife. Me and Ken were very close.

Geri:

Ken says "The Granddaughters are beautiful. You are doing a good job. He is proud of all of you.
So Please let go of the guilt now".

Terry:

I feel like I have just put down a heavy ruck sack. Thank you so much Geri I can't believe it.

Geri:

I also have your dad here Alan, saying "Sorry I couldn't be there for you son". Does this mean anything?

Terry:

I never knew my father, so I would not know whether he is dead or alive.

Geri:

He showed me red roses for November! Is that your birthday?

Terry:

Yes!

Geri:

Please take your father's apologies and your father-in-law's gratitude with you today Terry. I know this has helped you.

Terry:

I feel emotional and much lighter, thank you.

NUMBER 2

Geri:

Hi Jenny, come in!

Jenny:

Thank you Geri.

Geri:

Martin is here, who is Martin?

Jenny:

"OMG, that's my husband he died last year"

Geri:

Did he hang himself?

Jenny

(Crying) "Yes"

Geri

He is sending you and Tony his love!

Jenny

Tony is my son.

Geri

Martin is laughing saying "Happy Birthday"

Jenny:

It's my Birthday today!

The reading continued for an hour leaving Jenny ecstatic and happy!!

I would just like to add that Geri has on numerous occasions given me messages from my son Calum, who passed away in 2002. Also other family members and friends, which in turn has personally given me great comfort.

Geri is an amazing, gifted medium and brings great happiness and joy to many who seek her advice and knowledge. Personally, I would like to thank Geri from the bottom of my heart for all the treasured times we have spent together over the years, and I am honoured to call her one of my true friends.

A truly amazing lady!

Chapter 42

Quotes

Sathya Sai Baba appeared to Andy one night and said the following:

"I am the stem of the flower
you are my petal
I give you strength to cling
to me
To grow in all strength
and to flourish in all beauty
Take the water from the stem
The water is my love
Call upon me and
I shall guide and protect you"

Andy always comments that he tries to maintain this in his daily life.

KNOTS

Man is tied in many knots
He is like a piece of rope stretching
to breaking point!
If he opens to divine love
The knots will soften and finally disperse
The rope will slacken and
become more flexible
All tension and stress shall ease
and finally disappear
Then gradually, the rope shall turn
into a golden thread.

Long Line Alkaline
"Light of Love"

Why do you not know God?
Why do you not feel God?
You have been given the torch
of true happiness and bliss
But you must supply the batteries
the batteries of Love

This is a poem received in a meditative state
by Andrew McKellar.

If you want to know what your

true beliefs are,

Take a look at your actions

*"One meet's one's destiny
often on the road
one takes to avoid it"*

- **French Proverb**

Unseen Friends

There are eyes that watch over us
every single day
There are eyes that watch over us
while we are here to stay
We are given guidance
in our lives from unseen friends
If we link to power within
we can know our unseen friends
If we link to power within
more guidance shall we gain
If we look back over many years
We surely can say

How did we make it
through the difficult times?
Was there guidance along the way?

This poem received in a meditative state
by Andrew McKellar

PAPER

If you set light to a piece of paper
it shall burn from one end to the other
If it is blown about in the wind,
or rain pours down upon it,
it will go out half burnt
For God's love to burn through you,
know that his hand holds you close to him;
know that with his love and protection he will
shelter you
Always have ultimate faith in his omnipresence,
and his love will burn
through you and cleanse you
And cleanse you with the fire of love

This is a poem received in a meditative state
by Andrew McKellar

Wave of the Hand

As the devotees wait for him
to appear from the ashram
As the sun goes dim
As the Indian sun goes down
He appears from his ashram
in his orange gown
A glow around him
to light up the place
A loving smile on every face
as he moves out through the crowds
Blessing people as he moves around
With a twirl of his wrists the vibhuti sheds
The healing he gives, the smile on his face
The power of his eyes so filled with grace
"I know you all" we hear him say
"not even a thought can go astray"

I shall be there in your hour of need
as a guide and protect you, you shall see
Just one thought to me, a cry for help
Baba is there to help you out"

21 January 1990
Andrew McKellar

Vibhuti, sacred ash manifested

by

Sri Sathya Sai Baba
and given to devotees
as a sign of grace and healing

BAREBACK

I ride bareback in the black hills
The black hills of my ancestral tribe
I ride bareback in the black hills
As my heart beats to memories of pride
I feel the spirit of the sun
That shines through way up high
I reminisce over my people
As tears well in my eyes
A proud race of Indians we once were
At peace with the spirit life
A proud race of Indians – yes, we were
Filled with the spirit of light
Peace in the tribes, peace on the land
The spirit of life lending a hand

At one we felt, peace in the mind
At one we felt, filled with pride
Our Tepees stood tall,
our fires glowed bright
Finding the love of our spiritual light
I feel inside the strength we planned
I feel my ancestors roaming the land
Sometimes I hear their ghostly calls
My ancestors calling the chants of old
I sit on a rock, I call out loud
I ask the Great Spirit
To make us proud

Andrew McKellar

SCEPTICS

The medical profession will scoff
The medical profession will whinge
The medical profession will laugh
The medical profession will cringe
They say that healing is nonsense
but what do they really know
About the power of healing
The power that freely flows
In their ignorance of
darkened, closed minds,
They slander and mock – try to scare
I smile to myself as I watch them
I smile as they pull out their hair

They are on a mission of love
To fight that greater force
The power of unconditional love

Yes, this power does more than they say
In infinite ways every day

In time foolish sceptics shall see
Spiritual healing works
Eternally

Andrew McKellar
24 March 2003

Simply Divine

Down through the ages we have been taught that God is something 'outside' ourselves. In many religious practices, people have had encrusted into their minds that God is something to fear.

The time has come when people are awakening. After centuries of ignorance and fear, people are awakening to Spirituality; awakening to the reality that everything that breathes, everything that lives, is God. So yes, you yourself are God. You are divine by nature. God resides within your very being.

Our responsibility is to realise this, to nurture, to know God within.

We must learn to forgive others, even those who do wrong to us.

We must cultivate love and compassion for all forms of life.

Love is the key to awakening the God within. Not selfish love, by loving that which you want to love.

Once you awaken to the divine within, you shall awaken to the divine in others, thereby seeing life in a different light. Your state of consciousness rises to a higher level. Thereafter you slowly become cleansed in spirit, mind and body.

Once man awakens to this truth, the dark pits of

illness and disease shall be filled with love and harmony. By banishing the bate of illness, negative force cannot take hold. Ignorance, jealousy, envy, revenge, hate, desire for selfishness, greed and other forms of negative mind activity slowly dissolve in the water of love and knowledge.

You are divine. Realise this truth. If you say this baby girl is mother, people would not understand. The baby girl shall grow into a woman one day and become a mother. Grow in the knowledge that you are divine and, as you grow, you shall realise divine qualities.

And, finally, the child of ignorance shall be the Mother of Knowledge.

God aware
God knowing
God realized

Received in a meditative state by Andrew McKellar

TESTIMONIALS OF PATIENTS ATTENDING THE HEALING SANCTUARY WHO HAVE GIVEN THEIR PERMISSION FOR THE DETAILS TO BE WRITTEN IN TURN TO HELP OTHERS

Cancer Patients

Brian

Received healing for cancer. After seeing consultant in April, it was discovered that he had no re-growth whatsoever of cancer cells.

Cured.

Alan

Having had an operation for cancer and receiving a detailed check-up, it was discovered that he had re-growth in his back. He received healing.

Cured.

Gayle

Breast/ovarian cancer/lump in neck.

After 6 weeks there was just one tiny speck left on lung.

At the next check-up, completely cured.

Fit and well and returned to work.

Carole

Ovarian cancer – 2 years symptoms.

GP kept telling her it was her age and brushed it off. She eventually insisted on taking a blood test and the results confirmed she did indeed have cancer.

They offered her chemo, but she refused and came for healing. After 5 sessions she was cured.

Then her sister was found to have Grade 3 cervical cancer. She had 4 weeks before they would operate. In the meantime she decided to see Andy also and came for treatment.

This lady too was cured.

Also, she had previously been told she could not conceive, but since having the healing she is now the proud mother of a bouncing baby boy, which she is thrilled about, naturally.

Her mother also came for treatment for cancer and was cured.

Then there was the son who broke his wrist one weekend and came to see Andy, as the hospital refused to plaster it as too swollen.

Andy gave him healing and he was using the hand on the Monday morning. On returning to the hospital it was discovered that indeed the break had healed.

Kim – USA

Kidney and lung cancer. Cancerous lump in neck and stomach. This was secondary cancer.

After 6 weeks, 1 tiny speck on lung left.

Next visit: nothing. Completely cured. Fit and well and

returned to work.

Les

Prostate cancer – catheter – blood abnormal. Chronic sciatica. He was told nothing could be done and would have the catheter for the rest of his life. They would not carry out an operation.

After a few visits for healing, completely restored to good health. No cancer, no catheter, no tablets. Blood returned to normal.

Cured and very active.

G.P.

He was suffering with fluid retention – after secondary cancer of prostate. He decided against an operation after he had carried out his own research and did not wish to go down the route of having chemotherapy or radiotherapy. Instead, he decided that after hearing about Andy he would attend his clinic for healing.

Afterwards he underwent a CAT Scan and an MRI, and it was found that there were no signs of the disease whatsoever, or any other symptoms.

He was cured. Yet again another success.

When Andy asked him where he would go in the event of any future illness, he stated categorically that he would definitely attend Andy's clinic in the first instance, and not NHS.

Food for thought!

Matt

Large lump in his neck. Pains in stomach.

It was diagnosed that he was suffering with constipation. Eventually it was found to be a tumour.

After healing, he was cured. No sign of the tumour or the lymph nodes.

Alison – USA

Breast cancer. Refused to have operation due to the fact that she had a poor immune system and felt that it would be under threat if she took the usual channel. Having heard of Andy, she decided to come over and have a few healing sessions with him.

On her return to USA she was shocked to find out that in fact she had it in both her breasts, and this in itself would have posed an even bigger threat to her health than she at first thought. However, on examination it was found that she had no signs of cancer whatsoever in either breast. Her blood tests were normal.

She had followed her own instinct, which was to have healing by Andy, and it proved to have been a very successful trip to the UK.

As you can imagine, she was over the moon, so to speak.

Gentleman
USA

He had heard about Andy whilst in India, and decided to visit him as he was suffering with prostate cancer. PSI extremely high.

After healing, PSI back to normal. No cancer.

Cured.

Ann
Majorca

12cm tumour in bowel. This lady refused an operation and had healing over a two and a half week period and then flew to the UK, where she received further healing over a short period.

Her daughter had given her chemotherapy tablets each day, but she decided not to take them and continued down the road of healing.

Then the specialist insisted on operating and found no cancer whatsoever. The doctors were shocked, also the oncologist.

Cured – fit and well.

Carole

Tumour in chest. Form of Hodgkinson's lymphoma.

Medical profession said that it was slow growing.

Decided to see Andy before having operation.

A CAT Scan was carried out after 2 weeks and it was found that the tumour had completely vanished. Consultant amazed.

Fit and well.

Lindy

Majorca

12cm tumour in bowel. After 20 days in UK, it had shrunk to 5cm. Returning for healing, it had completely disappeared. When operating, nothing to be found at all.

Doctors and oncology unit now sending patients to Andy.

Sue

This lady was bedbound for 18 months. The medical profession decided to scan, as she was in great pain. It was discovered that in fact she had a tumour at the base of her spine.

Upon having healing sessions, she began to feel much better and the pain gradually went. Then the next step was to try and stand up from her wheelchair. This she did and then started to walk across the room.

Sue is now free of the tumour, does not need a wheelchair and has been restored to good health. In her own words, "it's a miracle!"

The power of healing.

Les

Cancer. Malignant melanoma. Nymph glands removed. It was explained to him that he had about two years to live.

Cured.

Nine years later – still here! Specialist amazed. Working full time and in the best of health.

Warren

Prostate cancer – Severe depression. Diagnosis: very short time to live. Depression disappeared after first healing. PSI returned to normal.
Regained complete health.
Cured.

Dr Steven James

Diagnosed with large mass on liver. Nothing could be done by the medical profession. After only two sessions the mass disappeared completely. His colleagues at Southampton General Hospital were amazed.
He had his life back!

Gentleman

Suffered with a growth on the top of his head for many years, but the consultant could do nothing about it.
After a few sessions it completely disappeared.

MULTIPLE SCLEROSIS

Sandra

Having had to use a walking frame for the last nine years as the illness was progressing, causing her to become depressed, it was decided that she should attend the

Nirvana Healing Sanctuary for some spiritual healing. Sandra was fully aware that it would possibly take time for the illness to be eradicated. Gradually over the next few weeks her balance was restored and depression was such that she no longer needed to take tablets. After a couple of weeks, she was already recovering and within a 4-month time scale she became free of the illness.

The power of Spiritual Healing had indeed taken place! Now Sandra is recommending everyone to experience the power of spiritual healing for themselves if they have health problems.

Sherry

Again an MS sufferer, for the past 20 years, and had severe problems when trying to walk and used a frame with great difficulty.

After receiving healing for 4 months she came into the Sanctuary with no frame, laughing, twirling around in absolute delight and hailing Andy as a miracle man! The happiness was infectious!

Her blood test showed that it had returned to normal. The specialist was absolutely amazed!

Vicky
MS

Severe symptoms – after a few sessions there was a total transformation as she regained her health again through spiritual healing.

HEART PROBLEMS

Nick
27 years old
Heart attack, plus angina.

He was informed by the specialists that he had in fact been born with a rare heart condition, whereby it had not grown specifically during his life and was the major factor causing the heart attack. He was informed that this was going to be his way of life from now on.

His life just stopped. His condition was such that he could hardly walk, and when bending he was totally aware that he could have an attack at any time. A frightening experience for such a young man, who thought he was physically fit and had been involved in sports from a very young age. Medically he was taking 67 tablets a day.

Almost 1 month after receiving healing, there was no angina. His heart regenerated and had repaired to normal. He did not require to take any more tables.

His consultant was stunned!

SEVERE BACK PAIN

Jane

Walking with a frame due to severe back pain. Consultant said there was nothing that could be done.

After healing – one week later, no sticks or frame.

Three weeks later – had returned to good health.

Consultant amazed.

Matt

Suffering with spinal problems and paralysis from waist down, gradually creeping into his arms and chest.

After healing – crutches not needed.

Then after a few more sessions he returned to good health. His feelings came back to his legs, arms and chest and he was standing upright and confident within himself.

I saw this young man, and it was miraculous the change in him. He was cured.

Lee

Chronic back pain, severe shooting pains for over 10 years. He had spinal surgery, MRI and cat scans, and he was still suffering. Lee was at his wits' end so to speak, just wanting to be able to feel normal again and free from pain. He was now wheelchair bound.

After some healing sessions he was cured at long last and has completely turned his life around, thanks to Andy.

Vince

Having had five operations on the base of his spine and still in chronic pain he decided to attend the Sanctuary.

After healing, the chronic pain disappeared. His spine recovered and he is now free of any problems associated with these operations.

He is now leading a normal life.

Freda

Severe spinal injury. In great discomfort.

After 7 minutes' healing: cured.

Steve

Using crutches and in total agony due to back problem.

After 20 minutes in the chair, he began to stand up slowly and the pain was easing. His legs were not stiff any more and he began walking.

12 hours later when he returned to the sanctuary after healing, he was totally cured.

Terry

Spondylosis of neck. Absolutely rigid. Could not move in any direction. Told that he had to get used to the idea that he would be unable to move his neck again.

After healing, totally cured.

Alan

He had suffered a trapped nerve at the base of his spine for over 30 years and could not use his hands properly, causing great discomfort. He was even unable to pick up a pen on the desk.

The nerve released after a few healings and returned to normal and he could then pick up the pen with his fingers. Truly amazing – cured.

Lady

Degeneration of hip and lower back problem after fall. On sticks. Suffered for about 3 years.

After 1 session, 1 week later – no sticks, walking upright - Cured.

Bruce
USA

Had 5 operations on spine. Suffering with Crohn's disease and diabetes.

All symptoms disappeared. Completely cured.

Mick

Base of spine extremely painful. Unable to stand upright. After healing: Standing straight.

No pain whatsoever after 20 minutes. Cured.

Fay

Damaged knee. Very painful. Suffering with arthritis. After 1 session – pain gone.

After 6 weeks, arthritis cured.

Beryl

Arthritis in knees for over 2 years. Needing replacement surgery.

After healing – no operation – returned to good health.

Trevor

Arthritis in back. Would be in a wheelchair in the foreseeable future.

After 10 sessions, cured. Free of pain in back and hands.

Such a relief for him as he runs his own business and needs the use of his hands.

Leanne

10 years arthritis – extreme pain. Medication 8 tablets a day.

Cured. No medication. Back to work.

Lisa

Cyst on ovaries. Told there was nothing at all which could be done for her.

After 5 sessions and 2 scans, there was no sign at all of the cyst and she regained full health – cured.

VARIOUS ILLNESSES

Steve – doctor
Southampton General Hospital
Renal Failure – extremely serious condition.

There was nothing which could be done for this young man.

Taking it into his own hands so to speak, he came to the Sanctuary and regained his health fully to this day. His blood returned to normal and he is back working again as a doctor helping others.

He had studied medicine for 5 years previous to his illness and therefore knew exactly what would have happened to him.

His comment: would always approach spiritual help before going to NHS.

Gail

Lung failure on oxygen.

After few sessions walked in with no oxygen mask and stating that she was off it for at least 8 hours a day. Most definitely carrying on with seeing Andy in the future.

Her Consultant was utterly amazed at her improvement.

Dave

Cyst – 7 years on his neck.

Disappeared completely after 3 sessions.

David's wife

Frozen shoulder – after one treatment only cured.

Gentleman

Frozen shoulder. On steroids. Chronic sciatica.

Cured.

Ian

Frozen shoulder. 1 session only.
Cured.

Les

Chronic sciatica. On walking sticks. On pain killers.
After few sessions no sticks; no tablets. Could touch his toes and delighted at outcome.
Cured

Male

Type 2 Diabetes – taking insulin regularly every day.
Cured – off insulin.

Harry

Kidney stones – After 55 operations, 450 stones and taking 16 Pethidine tablets a day to ease the pain, the consultant decided to operate and discovered he also had prostate cancer. It was decided that they would not operate as he was 82 years of age and sent him away to await his time.

Having heard of Andy he decided to book an appointment, and was indeed overwhelmed when after a number of healings it was discovered that the cancer had gone and the stones in his kidney had disappeared. He regained full health and never needed to take any more pills for pain. Totally cured.

Harry was truly overjoyed and I had the pleasure of meeting him personally and hearing his story.

Fran
No feeling in left leg, dragging when walking. Using stick.
1 week later walking unaided. 3 weeks later – cured.
Specialist amazed.

Pat
Frozen shoulder. Hospital suggested operation which she declined after treatment.
Cured.

Sue
Frozen shoulder.
Cured.

Holly
Frozen knee and leg from joint. On steroids.
Cured. 10 min. session.

Bobby
Carpal Tunnel Syndrome
A very severe case in both hands. She was advised to undergo an operation and a date was booked. However, she decided to see Andy. It was completely the right decision and her fingers were healed and the operation was cancelled. In turn

it meant that she could carry on with her career, which involved her using her hands to a great extent.

In her words: It was a miracle!

Bobby also had her dog treated by Andy for a tumour on its leg. Completely cured.

PSORIASIS, ECZEMA, AND DERMATITIS

Lady

Very severe case: had suffered for 36 years and it was all over her body. Causing great distress to her and in turn she was suffering from bouts of depression.

Cured – Her specialist was absolutely amazed. Her skin gradually improving over time and the scarring disappeared altogether and she was absolutely delighted.

Katy

Suffering from osteoarthritis and psoriasis for over 10 years and feeling very uncomfortable when asked about her problem. Also she was extremely depressed and on medication.

Cured – Absolutely delighted with the outcome and gained her confidence at last, and no more embarrassing moments were ever going to happen again. A truly remarkable outcome.

Craig

Eczema – serious skin complaint.

Cured after 1 week of healing.

Gentleman

Suffered with fibromyalgia for many years; intense headaches; feeling lethargic. He was leading a very poor standard of life due to the illness.
After a few sessions his health returned to normal.
Cured.

Diane – Writer

Rear prolapse – due to have operation.
Received healing.
Attended consultant – operation cancelled.

These are just a very small sample of the diseases which have been overcome, and there are many more which Andy over the years has had great success with.

At this point, I should like to mention that Andy sees many young patients, from babies upwards, who have major health issues, and who also have experienced amazing healing where it was thought there was no cure at all.

Patients not needing a wheelchair or specialised equipment any more but being healthy, running, jumping and all that goes with good health. Truly amazing for these children.

Also, animals are very welcome at the Sanctuary. Again

here, the owners have experienced the full return of their beloved pet being cured and then leading much happier lives than before.

**DIANE'S PERSONAL DEDICATION IS
TO THE MEMORY OF HER SON
CALUM LEWIS CANNINGS
*6.6.66 – 12.10.02***

**"FOREVER IN OUR HEARTS
UNTIL WE MEET AGAIN"**

**With all our love
Mum, Greta and Tristan
Your loving sister and younger brother**

**Calum and Satya Sai Baba have been a great
inspiration to Diane whilst writing this book.**

Diane has written this book in association over the last 30 years with her associate Andrew McKellar, for whom she has the highest respect for in relation to his phenomenal healing gift and dedication to his patients.

It is a totally unbiased account of Andrew's life based on actual events which have taken place.

Diane's strong survivor instinct and motivated outlook on life have given her an edge when relating Andy's story over to others.

Her own beliefs have given her inner strength and a strong desire to achieve which has helped her deal with the challenges which have occurred within her own life pathway.

I am honoured to have been asked by Andrew McKellar to write this book. Over many years I have seen the miracles which have occurred through Andrew's healing hands and how indeed, he has given life back to those who had been devastated and totally consumed with their particular life-threatening problem.

To experience the happiness and joy when their outlook at times had been very bleak gives a warm glow in my heart. The fact that in many instances they are restored to their former selves is amazing, to say the least.

SATYA SAI BABA GUIDES AND HELPS
ANDREW ON HIS LIFE'S PATHWAY
AS INDEED,
HE HELPS ME EACH
and
EVERY DAY!

BLESSINGS – NAMASTE
LOVE ALL SERVE ALL
SATHYA SAI BABA QUOTE

Diane M Homer

ACKNOWLEDGEMENT

I would personally like to thank Diane B. Layley for her insight and help whilst writing this book. She herself is an author of poetry, verse and short stories. So very much appreciated.

IF YOU SHOULD WISH TO PURCHASE VARIOUS OTHER ITEMS WHICH ANDREW McKELLAR HAS ON LINE THEN PLEASE LOOK ON AMAZON

www.andrewmckellar.com

I WOULD HIGHLY RECOMMEND THAT YOU ALSO LISTEN TO HIS CD WHICH CAME ABOUT AFTER A VISITATION BY SATHYA SAI BABA TO ANDY AND IN TURN THE MUSIC PRODUCER CRAIG PRUESS, WHO ALSO HAD A SIMILAR EXPERIENCE AND SUBSEQUENTLY MADE CONTACT WITH ANDY.

TRULY ENCHANTING
Sacred chants of
THE GAYATRI
The True Rendition

Relaxing and inspiring when meditating, giving a wonderful calming energy wherever you may be

www.heaven-on-earth-music.co.uk

AVAILABLE TO PURCHASE ON LINE
The latest CD

TO BE HEALED

by

THE UK'S LEADING SPIRITUAL HEALER
ANDREW MCKELLAR

www.andrewmckellar.com

On a lighter note, I am sure you will be pleasantly surprised to hear how Andrew relaxes in his spare time singing and playing the guitar. His voice is very similar to that of Elvis Presley and he is a great performer on the stage and without prejudice I would state that he is one of the best I have ever seen.

In the Rock & Roll theme Andrew wears all the amazing jackets, shirts, shoes etc., as only a true artist would.

Andrew appears at many venues across the South of England including weddings etc.

As you can imagine he comes highly recommended and I know you would have a very memorable event. Therefore I am going to suggest that should you have an event coming up in the future at which something different would appeal, then let Andrew perform for you!

Why not call him on: 07814928345 or on You Tube:
Andy McKellar Rock'n' Roll.